DEADBEAT DADS

DEADBEAT DADS

A National Child Support Scandal

Marcia Mobilia Boumil
and Joel Friedman

PRAEGER   **Westport, Connecticut**

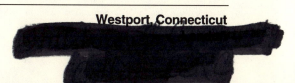

Library of Congress Cataloging-in-Publication Data

Boumil, Marcia Mobilia.
    Deadbeat dads : a national child support scandal / Marcia Mobilia
Boumil, Joel Friedman.
        p.   cm.
    Includes bibliographical references and index.
    ISBN 0–275–95125–1 (alk. paper)
    1. Child support—United States.   2. Child support—Government
policy—United States.   3. Desertion and non-support—United States.
4. Fathers—United States—Economic conditions.   I. Friedman, Joel.
II. Title.
    HV741.B693   1996
    362.7′1—dc20   95–34410

British Library Cataloguing in Publication Data is available.

Library of Congress Catalog Card Number: 95–34410
ISBN: 0–275–95125–1

First published in 1996

Praeger Publishers, 88 Post Road West, Westport, CT 06881
An imprint of Greenwood Publishing Group, Inc.

Printed in the United States of America

The paper used in this book complies with the
Permanent Paper Standard issued by the National
Information Standards Organization (Z39.48–1984).

10 9 8 7 6 5 4 3 2

To James and Gregory Boumil, and David, Peter and James Friedman, our next generation of dads. We hope their parents have shown the way.

Contents

Preface

In recent months, various political voices have indicated a strong desire to track down absent parents (usually fathers) who have absconded without fulfilling child support obligations to their biological or adopted children. The intent is to locate these parents and make them pay. In large part, this renewed interest in "deadbeat dads" has resulted from a recognition that social welfare programs, which pick up the tab for abandoned children, are contributing significantly to an ever-increasing federal budget deficit. In past years, the relative inattention toward pursuing absent parents in part resulted from the notion that it was as burdensome to regulate payment as it was simply to pay the bill. Of course, there were other reasons as well that the climate was not right for vigorously enforcing these moral as well as legal obligations: a father who deserted his children was a disgrace and to pursue him would further the insult.

Today we are all forced to come to terms with the reality that choosing not to pursue absent parents is a luxury that state and federal budgets can no longer afford. At the same time, the deadbeat epidemic has somehow become more of a moral issue than it was thought to be in the past, and the decision to pursue such delinquents is one that stirs up great controversy. This controversy centers on some of the same issues that contribute to parents leaving their children without providing for their welfare: in some cases, casual sexual practices result in large numbers of children being born out of wedlock, or of adulterous relationships, and/or to women who do not even know who the biological father is. In other cases, disruptions in families through divorce, separation, and cohabitation result in children being involuntarily separated from their biological parents, who are embittered by losing the custody and companionship of their children. If a child is moved away or drawn into a step-family, the noncustodial parent often feels left out and isolated. Too often those feelings result in an unwillingness to fulfill the financial obligations that would be expected.

While courts consistently refuse in any respect to condition the payment of support upon a parent's rights of custody or visitation, there is an undeniable correlation between the strength of an absent parent's social ties to his children and his willingness to fulfill his support obligations. A parent who is able to maintain a meaningful relationship with his children is simply more likely to keep up with his financial obligations. Today, more and more courts are urging warring parents to consider a shared custody arrangement that would give both parents substantial access to and influence over the lives of their children. While still the topic of much debate, many courts favor such an arrangement both because they believe that a continued relationship with both parents furthers the best interests of the children, and because they recognize that consistent payment of support is more likely to result.

What, exactly, is being done to further the campaign against deadbeat dads? The federal government has mandated that states, as a condition of continued receipt of federal funds to help support needy children, must put into place specific mechanisms to assist in locating absent parents and enforcing child support obligations. The laws require the states to provide for withholding wages, intercepting tax refunds, putting liens on property, and a number of other collection methods on behalf of children whose parents are delinquent. In addition, there have been great strides in refining the techniques available to prove paternity in cases of unwed or unacknowledged parents. Not long ago, the best that paternity tests could offer was to rule out the possibility that an "accused" man was the father of an illegitimate child. Technology in this area is advancing rapidly, and today paternity can be established with a high degree of accuracy.

In recent years, growing budget deficits and hard economic times have increased the incentive for enforcing child support obligations. At the same time, however, it is becoming increasingly apparent that in a large number of cases, there simply isn't enough money for an absent parent to maintain his own separate support and at the same time maintain the support obligations that the law requires. Many families are barely able to make ends meet with two incomes, and separate households add a great economic hardship. So at the very time that the political climate is right to clamp down on deadbeat dads, many find themselves escaping from their obligations out of necessity. To this dilemma there is no good answer.

Part of the recent reform in child support laws was the establishment of uniform guidelines for setting support, primarily to ensure consistency of awards. In large measure that goal has been met, but the cost is that the courts have less flexibility to consider the extenuating circumstances of individual defendants. This means that courts are required to establish support orders on the basis of income (primarily), with little ability to accommodate the absent father who wants to fulfill his obligations but simply cannot.

This book is not intended to operate in place of a lawyer. It is intended to educate the tens of thousands of single parents who are owed support or who are entitled to support but who have never been able to pursue their deserting mates. Its objective is to inform the reader about what is possible and what should be expected. More important, it is designed to empower the large number of individuals, primarily women, who are caught in the midst of overworked agencies, discouraging tales, and a lack of information that keeps them from acting on their own behalf.

If by chance or design a nonsupporting parent, a "deadbeat," reads this book, we hope that the information contained herein will lead to a reappraisal of the behavior that ultimately impacts most on the innocent victims of deadbeats—the children. It is they who carry the biological heritage of the offending parent and who suffer the effects of poverty, abandonment, and a discontinuity with their personal history.

Throughout this book, the names, occupations, ages, and location in the case studies have been changed to protect the interviewees.

Marcia Mobilia Boumil
Joel Friedman

1

The Deadbeat Epidemic: A New Generation of Neglected Children

CASE STUDY: TED

Sara and I lived together for three years after we graduated from college. You might say we were college sweethearts, of sorts. Unlike me, Sara was very clear about what she wanted: marriage and babies. She often said that she loved me, and I believe she did. In my own way I guessed I loved her, too, but I loved my ambitions more. Somehow I think I expected to graduate from college and take over as the CEO of some major company. I had no clue about what the real world was all about, but I knew I was determined to go out and get a piece of it.

By the time we had lived together for three years it was obvious to me how important the marriage-and-babies stuff was for Sara. So even though for me it was far too remote, I just couldn't bring myself to say things that I knew would hurt her. For months I played the part of being in a "couple relationship." We'd do things with other couples and we'd listen to them talk about building their lives together. Some had already gotten engaged. I could never participate, though, and I did everything possible to avoid the issue of marriage. I thought I was trying to protect Sara and I was sure that I didn't want to lose her, but I also didn't want to marry her.

After dancing around the subject for months, Sara was really pressuring me for a commitment and I finally had to tell her that I didn't love her the way I felt I should in order to get married. She did just what I expected: she got very upset and accused me of leading her on and taking the best years of her life while I worked to advance my career. And then she moved out. Even though we had really gotten along well together, she knew just what she wanted, and I wanted something very different—or so I thought.

Even after Sara and I were officially broken up, once in a while she would call me, or I would call her and we would talk, and maybe we'd go out to dinner or something. Nothing more. Even though I think we still loved each other, our differences were too great, and we both knew it.

One evening when I was feeling particularly lonely and frustrated, I called Sara and suggested that we get together. She was delighted to come over and we had a great evening. Sara ended up spending the night and, to my surprise, when it was all over she was able to say goodbye without a hassle. I thought it was great having someone like Sara to just be with once in a while without having to constantly be pressured about getting married.

It had been nearly two months since that night we spent together, with no contact in the interim, when out of the blue Sara called and announced matter-of-factly that she had missed two periods and was pretty sure that she was pregnant. Not only that, but she was happy about it and had every intention of going through with the pregnancy. She said that she would do anything I wanted to make us a happy family, but she also seemed to know that I would never buy into that.

I was beside myself with anger. I was sure that she had purposely not used birth control and probably even wanted this to happen. When I confronted her, she said that she hadn't expected to spend that night with me and thought I knew she didn't have any birth control. She said she also figured that if I really didn't want this to happen, I could have taken care of it. Can you imagine that? Here I spent three years trying not to hurt her feelings; we get together for one night with no strings attached, and then she turns around and does this? And on top of it, somehow I'm to blame? Well, no way. I'm not going to let this situation ruin my life. I made it clear that I had no interest in marriage and kids, and a pregnancy isn't going to tie me down. Let her get an abortion! It's been nearly a year and a half since that all happened. Sara has never asked me for anything. She went home to live with her parents, who are well able to support her and their grandson and seem happy to do it. But I am really confused. I don't know how to relate to Sara and the baby. And when I think about this whole mess, it's hard to forget that when I was a kid, my father never seemed to know how to relate to me. He and my mother were divorced when I was eleven years old because they never seemed to be able to see eye-to-eye on anything.

Back in the days of my own childhood, my father was never home much. His job kept him on the road most of the time, which seemed to be fine with him. He'd be home a couple of times a month and for holidays, and otherwise he'd always be working. My mom thought it was really important to have a stable home for me and my brother, so we'd stay put while dad was off living and working in other places. Whenever dad got a new job opportunity he would always take it, regardless of where he had to relocate.

Even when dad wasn't traveling, he still never had time for us. Sometimes my brother or I would ask him to come to a baseball practice or maybe just go out to a movie or something, but he would never have time. He just said he had to work. And what little time he did spend at home, he and my mom were always arguing. Finally, my mom asked him to leave for good, and it didn't seem to make a lot of difference to him one way or the other. I really missed him a lot, though.

The idea that he and mom were split up forever really didn't sink in until I was much older. I just seemed to have no clue about what having a father was all about. I still saw him on holidays and I always looked forward to seeing what new things he would buy. He said that buying new cars and stereos and clothes and stuff was what success was all about. Mom had worked hard, too, but she never seemed to be able to get those extras, so if dad would get me a new radio or something, it made me feel important. I always knew that when I grew up I would make sure that I had those things, too, so my dad would be proud of me.

Even though I usually try to put the whole thing about Sara and the baby out of my mind so I can concentrate on my work, I find that I'm often distracted by it. As you might expect, my mom and dad have different ideas about what I should do. Mom is dying to have a grandchild and thinks that I should visit Sara and the baby and work out something where I can be a father even if I don't want to get married and relocate. She sends the baby presents behind my back. Dad, on the other hand, feels that I was manipulated into this situation and advises me to stay away from Sara and "her" baby and go on with my life as I had planned.

I recently went on vacation to visit my father and his new wife, and I was about a four-hour drive from Sara and the baby. This was the perfect chance for me to get to see the baby and, frankly, I was curious about what he looks like, and what it might feel like to be around him. And even though a part of me was still very angry at Sara, another part of me still felt very connected to her. I was also worried about giving Sara the wrong message. I didn't want her to mistake my feelings of curiosity for feelings of love. I certainly didn't want her to think that I was about to involve myself with her and the baby in a regular way. I might be willing to come around on holidays or something, but I certainly wasn't going to be tied down. And then, of course, there was the financial part of it. The last thing in the world that I needed was a financial commitment that I couldn't handle.

I found myself torn between spending almost a day of my precious vacation going to visit Sara and the baby, and putting the visit on hold until I had a better sense of what might happen and what I really wanted. Did I have any feelings for this child at all? Was I really the father, given the circumstances of the conception? Was I so hurt and angry about how Sara used me that I could never forgive her and have any kind of relationship with the child? Was I just so frightened of the financial liability that could disrupt all of my career goals and the things I was taught to really value in life?

Or was I just another irresponsible and selfish man who was more concerned with himself than the child he fathered? All of this was tearing at me while I was trying to enjoy a vacation. Totally confused, I turned to my father for some guidance.

Before I could even explain to dad some of the things that I was thinking about, he made it absolutely clear what he thought I should do. His advice was for me to enjoy my vacation and not spoil it by going to see the girl who used me and tried to wreck my life. He said that it was not my fault or my responsibility that things happened as they did, and the more I got involved, the more difficult it would be for me to continue on with my own life. Besides, he pointed out, how was I so sure that I was the father anyway? A woman who could do this to me was capable of doing anything. He put his arm around me and gave me one of those man-to-man type hugs as a way of accentuating his point. Getting that type of affection from him was so rare that I couldn't possibly carry on any further discussion about visiting Sara and the baby. His position was very clear: a man should spend his time pursuing his career and earning a good living. Nothing should be allowed to stand in the way of success, not even his own child.

This, of course, was not a new message to me, as I had learned it firsthand just by being his son. I remember one time being really bothered by something that had happened in school. I called my dad because it was something that you really couldn't talk to your mother about. I was so upset on the phone that it was hard to explain what had happened. Just then, another call came in for him and he abruptly interrupted and told me that he had to take a business call. He never did call back and it became so clear to me what his priorities were. I knew what I had to do to earn his respect.

I never did get in touch with Sara. I've asked my mom to stop sending gifts to the baby until I figure out what kind of relationship, if any, that I want with him and Sara. I'm grateful that they're well cared for, and I'm glad that they don't need me. Once in a while I think about them, and how the baby must be growing, but mostly I stay buried in my work. For once my dad has actually taken an interest in me, if only to help me stay focused and not get distracted from my career goals. My dad's interest is really important to me, and I'm going to do everything I can to hold on to it.

DISCUSSION OF TED'S CASE

Ted's case is typical of the young, unmarried couple who is faced with an unintended pregnancy. If the couple does not marry and the woman chooses to bring her pregnancy to term, it is not unusual for her to raise the child within her own family of origin. In this case, Sara's family is apparently supportive of her and her child and are willing to assist in the care and maintenance of both of them.

It is not unusual that Sara would not pursue Ted for child support. It is estimated that barely one-quarter of mothers who were never married to their child's father will ever even receive an award of child support, which says nothing about the rate of collection. Furthermore, the amount of the average award is far lower than that which would be expected by other eligible mothers. Statistics indicate that the average unwed mother who actually received child support in 1989 got just over $150 per month.

Not surprisingly it is also not unusual that Ted would not seek any visitation of his child. Many such unwed fathers do not think of themselves as fathers at all, much less deadbeats. They did not intend fatherhood; they did not choose fatherhood. And having never signed on to having a child, they feel no obligation to fulfill any paternal obligation. This, of course, is exacerbated if the mother cannot definitively identify the father of her child and he is left to wonder about his paternity. Thus for these children the deadbeat dad is not one who has absented himself from his child's life—he never existed at all.

CHILD SUPPORT'S UNDERPINNINGS

Prior to the 1960s a man's obligation to support his wife and children was rarely questioned. Fewer children were born out of wedlock, and fewer couples divorced. The family's social structure was more rigid, as the roles of men and women were better defined and less easily challenged: men went to work, women cared for the children. Few women had the wherewithal (economically or emotionally) to walk away from an unhappy marriage. And rather than receiving the social support that she might get today, a woman could expect to feel isolated and disgraced. By the same token, the male role of patriarch required him to support his wife and children, and society recognized little excuse for his failing to meet those obligations. This does not mean, of course, that husbands did not cheat on their wives or that children were not born out of wedlock. What it does mean was that society imposed and watched over the moral obligation of a man to provide for his family.

Interestingly, the standards imposed by society's mores were rarely enforced by the law. Absent parents were rarely pursued. Paternity was rarely established. And even if the child support obligation was established by law, an absent father could all but walk away from it. Why was this so? In large part, the federal program of Aid to Families with Dependent Children (AFDC) was the reason. AFDC is a social program of support, primarily for single mothers with dependent children. Some attempts were made, of course, to get such families off of AFDC by finding absent fathers and making them meet their child support obligations. There was little incentive to do so, however, since whatever support was received would merely be offset against AFDC entitlements. There was also the argument that it would take as much money to pursue deserting parents as it would simply to pay AFDC. There was even the suggestion that pursuing absent fathers actually would harm the family, both because it was "inconvenient" for custodial mothers to pursue unwilling fathers and because it might actually drive away unmarried fathers—those who maintain a social tie but do not meet the financial obligation.

In the 1970s and 1980s, Congress enacted sweeping new legislation to reform child support enforcement, primarily as a result of the increasing cost of the federal AFDC program (see chapter 5). In large measure, the legislation acknowledged changed social

values, the breakdown of the family, and the realities of single
parenting, step-families and out-of-wedlock children. It attempted
to balance the needs of the social welfare system with an understanding of why absent parents abdicate their child support obligations.

CHILD SUPPORT GUIDELINES

All states have now enacted child support guidelines which
means that the minimum level of support that an absent parent must
pay for the support of dependent children is set by the court (or by
agreement of the parties) in accordance with the guidelines.
Generally the courts take into account the incomes of both parents
and assign support on the basis of gross income of the absent parent
up to a maximum level. The percentage increases with the number
of children. Other financial obligations are considered, but for the
most part child support is considered to be a primary obligation and
there is little leeway for the parties or the court to alter the
obligations under the guidelines.

> Susan and Dan were married for less than a year when
> Susan became pregnant with their child. The marriage
> was shaky from the beginning and Susan and Dan
> separated only a few months after the child was born.
> A divorce followed and Dan was ordered to pay a
> reasonable amount of support for the child. Two years
> later, Susan was living with another man whom her
> child called "Daddy." Dan did exercise his rights of
> visitation, but when Susan remarried it became more
> and more difficult for Dan to play an active role in his
> child's life.

The questions that this scenario raises are more provocative
than the answers that are available. If a parent is deprived of
custody, does this diminish his financial obligations to the
child(ren)? To what extent should child support reflect the actual

tie that an absent father has with his family? Should a noncustodial parent whose child is moved away (and to whom visitation is thus limited) be required to provide the same level of support? And is a mere biological connection to a child sufficient to impose an obligation of support anyway?

The purpose of the child support guidelines was primarily to standardize the level of support that noncustodial parents would be required to pay for their children. This prevents individual judges from imposing wide variations in awards, which otherwise leads to an appearance of unfairness. Prior to the widespread enactment of such guidelines, it was common for two similarly situated men to have seemingly very different support obligations to their dependent children. (Of course, individual circumstances vary widely and each case is considered separately in establishing a reasonable level of support.) The challenge that faced the legislative reform was to strike a balance between the need to accommodate individual circumstances and the need for objective fairness and uniformity. One of the significant advantages to uniform (and thus predictable) awards is that it maximizes the incentive to settle cases rather than go to court: the parties know ahead of time what the court will award.

A disadvantage of the uniformity of guidelines is that there is no accommodation for variations in social ties and moral obligations. *A noncustodial parent who retains joint legal and/or physical custody (see chapter 6) is usually more willing to contribute to the support of his children than is an absent parent whose tie to his children has been severed.* Another wrinkle appears if the custodial parent marries or cohabits with someone else. Many parents are loathe to contribute substantial support for children who recognize another adult as mother or father.

While women's return to the work force in large numbers has greatly contributed to the ability of married couples to separate, economic conditions in recent years have prevented many separated parents from fulfilling child support obligations even when they are inclined to do so. For example, a man who lives independently from his children and their mother (perhaps with another woman or step-family) is often barely making ends meet with his own living expenses, and simply has little money available to contribute to the support of his own children. Indeed, it is speculated that the recent slight downward trend of divorces is once again a result of economic circumstances: many families cannot afford the luxury of separate households. In those cases where a break is made anyway, men who default in their support obligation often do so because they see no alternative. The current guidelines are often too inflexible to allow for necessary modifications. The result is that many low-income fathers stay hopelessly in arrears, affecting their social ties to their children as well.

In a day and age in which many separated couples cannot both maintain separate households and meet their children's needs, children produced through casual and uncommitted relationships rarely stand a chance for having their economic needs met. Indeed, the needs of more and more children are on a collision course with the limitations of the social programs that are called upon to pay the bills. At issue today is whether stricter enforcement of child support obligations of deserting fathers will help solve the overall problem.

The rationale for enforcing (or not enforcing) child support obligations has shifted dramatically over the years. The hands-off approach of the 1950s and 1960s has steadily moved toward an emphasis in the 1980s and 1990s on the moral culpability of a delinquent father, whose unwillingness to meet child support obligations deems him irresponsible and immoral. There may be a number of reasons for this, including the increased visibility and political strength of various women's groups whose interest in making deadbeat dads pay is obvious. No doubt the conservative, anti-welfare federal administrations of the 1980s also contributed to the shift. What has probably had the greatest influence, however, is the reality that the ever-increasing burden on the state and federal social programs requires a change in policy. And when change is required, doing something—perhaps anything—is better than doing nothing. The result has evolved into what is now a sharp, even intense, preoccupation with pursuing absent fathers in order to demonstrate that society is "doing something."

Does it make sense to pursue men who father children and thereafter abdicate their social and economic obligations to them? In many cases it does. To the extent that absent parents maintain their social, moral, and economic obligations to their children, the damage is minimized. Even in those cases where the family ties are significantly disrupted (e.g., one parent moves far away) the financial contribution helps the children get a better start in life. And in those cases where economic support is possible, although perhaps a hardship for the absent parent, it makes sense to pursue these individuals and make them meet their financial obligations. Furthermore, as a practical matter, the money collected usually far exceeds the fees spent in pursuing such parents.

The more difficult questions arise in cases in which the so-called deadbeat dads simply don't have the resources to pay the child support awards ordered under the inflexible state guidelines.

> David and Joanne were divorced two-and-a-half years ago, leaving two children in Joanne's physical custody. David was awarded substantial visitation (weekends and two evenings per week), which he fulfilled regularly. The child support, however, was a problem from the start. His and Joanne's incomes together were barely enough to run their modest home. When David moved into his one-bedroom apartment, he was unable to pay both his own bills and give enough to Joanne to run the house. Joanne was unwilling to sell the house, which was the only asset that she was awarded, primarily because the mortgage payments were less than would be the rent on an apartment adequate for herself and two children. David's search for a higher paying job was fruitless, and a second job would substantially reduce his time spent with the children. Joanne was advised that bringing David back to court would be expensive and probably wouldn't yield much anyway. Eventually David's

inability to maintain his child support obligations
affected his relationship with the children, as the bitterness between himself and Joanne was perpetuated
by this continuing dispute. Visits were consumed by
the ongoing economic crisis, and the children's limited
understanding of what it was all about left them with
a degraded image of their father in their minds.

This situation underscores the tension between standardized
guidelines—which are designed to ensure that the children are
provided for financially through predetermined, uniform awards—
and the need to accommodate individual circumstances when there
are limited resources available.

CHANGING RATIONALE FOR CHILD SUPPORT OBLIGATIONS

Certainly an absent parent's ability to pay for the support of his
children is a major consideration in setting the child support
obligation. It is also clear that many delinquent parents who are in
arrears are those who are substantially unable to make ends meet.
But there is also another significant group of deadbeat dads who
willfully refuse to pay: those who do not accept that there is a moral
obligation to do so.

Ginny left Stan more than five years ago after he found
out that she was having an affair with Peter. Ginny
and Stan were never married, but he thought they had
made a commitment to each other and was devastated
when Ginny left. There was a court battle over the
custody of their five-year-old daughter, but, without
being married to Ginny, Stan was advised that he
didn't stand a chance. Eventually the custody was, in
fact, awarded to Ginny, although Stan was given
liberal visitation. He was also given a significant bill
for child support, most of which has never been paid.

Ginny married Peter soon after and Stan decided to
move out of state. The child maintains some contact
with Stan, but it is limited by the distance. Recently
Stan has also married and is planning a family with his
wife. He makes less and less effort to pursue visitation
with his daughter, and is grateful that Ginny makes
little effort to pursue support.

It is difficult not to observe that family ties and loyalties are less
binding today than they were even a generation ago and that many
individuals, for whatever reasons, feel less of a commitment to
maintain significant ties with their families. This is particularly
evident with adult children, who move around the country with
fewer qualms about leaving family behind than ever before. It is
also true, however, of parents who bring children into the world
and thereafter find that a continuing commitment to them is
inconsistent with other goals in their lives. This movement away
from traditional values has a significant effect on the evolution of
individuals who grow up and develop their own values about
family responsibility. The relationship between the deadbeat
epidemic and the movement away from traditional values is
apparent.

How does a decline in family ties affect the moral obligation of
a parent to provide for the continuing support of the children?
Individuals with less family loyalty are also likely to perceive
fewer obligations to the family. If a father cannot (or does not)
have a significant ongoing relationship with his children, does he
have an obligation of support? Does it matter whether he or
someone else is responsible for the absence of the relationship?
Interestingly, it is at the time of the greatest change in familial ties
and values that it has become necessary to pursue absent parents
with such vigor. Attempts to reconcile competing interests and
resolve the current dilemma have met with resistance, primarily
because a good solution has not presented itself. At best, there can
be a redefinition of what society's involvement should be in
pursuing absent fathers (or mothers, for that matter) whose social

and emotional ties to their children have been broken but whose financial contribution could be critical to the well-being of their children.

Among the many things that have changed from a generation ago is a phenomenal rise in the number of single-parent families as a result of both illegitimate births and divorce. Out-of-wedlock fornication is rarely even prosecuted as a crime, although it still remains illegal in many states. Nonmarital cohabitation and sexual relations have become commonplace. Under the standards of a generation ago, today's sexual conduct even among responsible adults would be considered promiscuous. The birth rate among unskilled, ill-prepared, and unwed teenagers is of a magnitude that threatens many of our cultural institutions.

Other relatively recent social changes also contribute to the overall picture. Today abortion is legal and, for the most part, available to many women. Contraception is more effective and more widely available, even to indigent men and women who do not want their sexual behavior to result in pregnancy. Another significant factor has been the AIDS epidemic, which has forced large numbers of people to rethink their lifestyles and sexual habits under a threat of dire consequences. Finally, the economic cost of supporting a child until the age of maturity has skyrocketed (currently estimated in the range of $100,000). Having an unwanted child is no longer just an inconvenience or even a disgrace; today the financial obligations can be staggering.

Yet another factor is the increased participation of men in the upbringing of children. A generation ago, a man's obligation was primarily focused on providing food, clothing, shelter, and other necessities of life. Women raised the children, usually with little active participation from men. Today there has been a dramatic increase in the amount and quality of time that many men spend with their children. As a result, a man's absence is a significant loss to the upbringing of his children, and not just to their economic well-being. At the same time, the loss of his custodial rights often results in great emotional loss to the man who has actively participated in the care of his children. Even the most indulgent fathers lose their position of cherished patriarch, and too many lose any meaningful relationship with their own children.

What is the nature of the financial obligation that an absent father owes to his children? Does "fault" on the part of either parent matter? And how much of society's resources should be delegated toward finding delinquent parents and making them satisfy their economic obligations to their children, particularly when their social ties are all but gone? One approach to answering these questions is to examine the rights that are available to absent fathers, unmarried or divorced, so as to determine whether they are consistent with the support obligations that are currently imposed.

THE RIGHTS OF A BIOLOGICAL PARENT

Numerous cases have found their way through all levels of the court system in which biological fathers (wed and unwed) have sought to assert their constitutional rights to care and companionship of their children. To the extent that the mirror image of child support is the right to maintain an ongoing relationship with the child (which, incidentally, is *not* the case) a biological father's rights to custody and visitation certainly merit consideration. The hallmark for child custody awards is always the "best interests of the child" (see chapter 6). This presumes, of course, that those contending for custody have a legal basis to do so. Among the many difficult questions that have arisen are those addressing the issue of whether a biological connection is sufficient to assert a legal claim.

The 1983 United States Supreme Court case of *Lehr v. Robinson* involved a biological father who sought to adopt his illegitimate child. At the time of the proceeding, the father had neither acknowledged the child as his nor had he established a paternal relationship with the child. The Supreme Court stated:

When an unwed father demonstrates a full commitment to the responsibilities of parenthood by "com[ing] forward to participate in the rearing of the child," his interest in personal contact with his child acquires substantial protection.... But the mere existence of a biological link does not merit equivalent constitutional protection. The actions of judges neither create nor sever genetic bonds. (463 U.S. 248 [1983])

In 1989, the Supreme Court again ruled on paternity rights in the case of *Michael H. v. Gerald D.,* which dealt with a child born to Carol D. and Gerald D. while the couple was married. Gerald was listed as the father on the child's birth certificate. However, a blood test revealed that there was a 98.07 percent likelihood that Michael H., a man with whom Carol D. had had an adulterous affair, was the child's father. The applicable state law provided that a child born to a married couple, living together, was "presumed" to be a child of the marriage. The Supreme Court upheld the state ruling, and Michael H. was denied the opportunity to prove his paternity, although the court intimated that under slightly different circumstances it might rule differently (see chapter 6).

Notwithstanding these Supreme Court decisions, there have been numerous cases in the lower courts that have addressed the paternity rights of fathers, wed and unwed, of children who are conceived or born outside of a traditional marital relationship. Under a great variety of circumstances, many such fathers have been granted substantial rights of custody and visitation. At the risk of oversimplification, the linchpin seems to be the nature of the role in the child's life that the biological father assumes (or perhaps, is allowed to assume) after the child is born.

So now the question arises: if a biological father is denied the opportunity to assert his rights of fatherhood, can he be forced to support a child whom he chooses not to acknowledge?

Deanna and Rick enjoyed a casual dating relationship for several months without any intention of making a permanent commitment to each other. They engaged in sexual relations only a few times before it became evident to both of them that they had no future together. Even when they did have sex, Rick tried to be careful to use reliable birth control. Deanna notified

Rick nearly three months into a pregnancy that she had conceived a child. Rick has never known whether it was accidental, but in any event Deanna agreed to an abortion. The social relationship between Rick and Deanna trailed off over the next months. Although Rick inquired several times about the abortion and offered to pay for it, Deanna never "got around to it," and eventually it became too late. A child was born, and Rick refused to acknowledge paternity or to provide child support.

The connection between the quality of the personal relationship that a biological father has with his child and his willingness to provide child support has been adequately documented. As yet, however, the law has been unwilling to reflect that issue in its support awards. In fact, it reflects just the opposite: discontent with custody or visitation is not a reason to withhold support. Moreover, the level of child support that a court will order is determined under local guidelines on the basis of ability to pay, and there is little leeway to even consider extenuating circumstances, much less the social relationship between the biological father and his child.

The unwillingness of the courts to recognize the obvious impact of continued social ties between parent and child may well stem from the court's inability to affect it in any meaningful way, any more than it can "fix" broken parental relationships. Unless a parent is unfit, courts always encourage liberal visitation, both because of the legal rights of the noncustodial parent and because the child support obligation is more readily met when social contact continues. But the cruel reality remains that a vast number of these children become the victims of poverty, welfare, and the lack of a social support system that they so desperately need to get a decent start in life.

Marianne met Glenn in a nightclub and ended up spending the night with him. Both had had too much to drink, and Marianne has little memory of what actually happened that night. At one point she even thought of trying to charge Glenn with rape, but she just wasn't certain enough about what actually happened that evening. Two-and-a-half months later she found out that she was pregnant, and a paternity test after the child was born revealed a 98.77 percent likelihood that Glenn was the father. Marianne worked as a waitress and was barely able to make enough money to even pay for child care, to say nothing of the fact that she was away from her child for most of the time. Eventually Marianne was so far into debt that she had to stop working and accept welfare in order to make ends meet. The welfare department thereafter pursued Glenn to support the child.

CONCLUSION

The issues surrounding the support of society's youngest generation are among the most complex social, legal, and economic concerns that face this country today. We are asked to find a solution for the sake of the children that emphasizes hope rather than assigns blame. But it is hard not to point fingers at those who seem to be responsible, even when it doesn't help the cause. The reality is that there are no good answers, and there's not enough money in the federal budget (with its ever-increasing deficit) to bite the bullet and just simply do what's best for the children. For many years we did just that, but today the economics of federal and state social support have spiraled out of control. No matter how important a social program is, the point comes at which it cannot continue to be funded; child support has become just such a program. As a result, we find ourselves in a quagmire of difficult questions and competing interests. The challenge that faces us is to sort through these complex issues and strike some sort of balance between moral dilemma and economic necessity.

2

Children of Divorce:
The Psychological Consequences
of Divorce and Absent Parents

CASE STUDY: ELIZABETH

I was eleven when my parents separated for the last time. No one who knew us was surprised: for as long back as I could remember they never got along. But for some reason I think we children were surprised, probably because we were so used to the way things were that we thought they wouldn't change. And maybe it was because kids are never really prepared for a major disruption that threatens their lives and their families and their security. But as I look back at it, it wasn't so much the breakup that I remember as being so hard; it was the way it happened. In fact, in the aftermath we actually had a little peacefulness for the first time.

For as many years of my life as I can remember my parents had fallen into a pattern that repeated itself once or twice each year. They would have a major argument, followed by my father leaving the next day and returning one to two weeks later after both had cooled off. At some point we learned not to ask anymore where he was and he would not call while he was away. We simply knew that he was "gone" and that he would reappear when he was "ready." Mom didn't like to talk about things, and as far as she was concerned there was nothing to talk about anyway.

Then at one point it just happened. What appeared to be the same pattern repeated itself in the late fall and a major argument was followed by Dad leaving. There was no discussion about where he was, but this time it was three weeks to the day before he returned. He walked in one day in the middle of the afternoon after we had returned from school. We probably exchanged some normal conversation about it being nice to see him and maybe what had been going on in his absence. I say "maybe" because I don't really remember anything remarkable about his return. Then around five o'clock (when Mom would be expected home shortly) he picked up his jacket and got up to leave. I wasn't particularly paying attention except that he turned to me and my brother and said casually, "You know that if you need me you can reach me at my mother's."

We both looked at him with what must have appeared to be a blank stare, but neither of us said a word. We had been trained well to be strong and nonreactive and, like everything else, we took it in stride. He proceeded to go, and afterward my brother and I exchanged a brief glance, and he, too, got up and left. We never spoke a word to each other about that day, but my guess is that he caught on more quickly than I.

I remember clearly the thoughts that raced through my head. "There's something wrong with his mother," I imagined. "She must need him." And then I became a little more realistic. "He's not ready to come back yet," I figured. "He needs more time." Somehow I must have managed to put it out of my head for the rest of the evening because I have no more memory of that night.

The next day, though, I remember vividly, as though it had happened yesterday rather than two decades ago. In the middle of the afternoon I returned from school and I was at home alone for the first time since the previous afternoon. As though with a mission, I went directly into my father's bedroom to inspect what was going on. Nothing immediately apparent was different, but I hesitated a moment before opening each of the drawers of his dresser. One by one I saw that each had been completely emptied out. Finally, in the bottom drawer there was a pair of old slippers and a stray sock. That was all. Nothing else. And then I noticed that the pictures that once stood on top were also missing. I didn't see that before. I turned next to the closet, as though I were a spy looking for anything. But I hesitated, almost afraid that my suspicions would be confirmed. And when I finally did look, indeed that's just what happened. Everything had been removed, and I mean everything. If there had been any doubt, the closet said it all.

For a moment I sat there dumbfounded and I was fighting to hold back the tears. After all, strong kids didn't cry. But this was a fight I was destined to lose, and within moments I was sitting on the floor crying like a baby. I sat there for more than an hour, processing multiple thoughts all at once. And again, the first ones were to defend the parents who weren't around to defend themselves. "Mom's very busy," I thought, "with a job and kids and all. She hasn't had time to tell us what's going on." As for Dad, I thought, "He's very emotional. This must have been very hard for him. He doesn't have the wherewithal to deal with us, too." And then there were the questions about what would happen next. Would we stay in the house? Would Dad come to visit? What would it be like without him? I suppose I should have known since he had already been gone for three weeks, but that was different. He was always coming back. But this time he wasn't and, needless to say, there had been no discussion about whether he would even come to visit.

Even while I was desperately trying to defend my parents, reality was forcing its way to the fore. "A man doesn't move out of a place that he's lived in for fifteen years by packing a suitcase. And he isn't sleeping on a couch for the night. This move was planned. It was intentionally carried out while we were away, probably at school. Both of them participated, and both of them knew that this moment would come. The kids had to figure it out eventually, and neither of them wanted to be around to help mop up the tears."

The story doesn't quite end there. Not only did neither parent ever say a word about Dad's leaving, but Mom managed to communicate the message that it wasn't something to be discussed with friends, neighbors, or even relatives. After all, what would the

Joneses have thought. When people would call on the telephone, we learned through example that they wouldn't be told that Dad doesn't live here anymore; we were to simply take a message and leave it for when he came around. One day a neighbor stopped to chat when Mom and I were in the driveway. She commented that she hadn't seen my dad in a while and Mom piped up, "He's been working late." Interesting, I thought, particularly since Dad hadn't worked in two years. And yet another time we were at a family gathering and someone asked me outright where my father was. I stumbled over my own words and finally mumbled, "I don't know."

One of the most difficult parts of this story was the loss of a friendship. Another girl in the neighborhood and I had been best friends since kindergarten and were in and out of each other's homes daily. We were truly best friends in a way that only two young girls can be. But she was also a neighbor and you can't tell a secret to a child without expecting the whole neighborhood to find out. So I never said a word. But eventually she kept asking about what was wrong and commenting that Dad wasn't around, and eventually it became easier to end the friendship than to keep making excuses. Within two months we had completely drifted apart. And I never said a word.

DISCUSSION OF ELIZABETH'S CASE

Elizabeth's account of her family breakup poignantly describes divorce as a process that begins long before the actual collapse of the family unit. Those who may think that divorce occurs when the court appearances begin and end must realize that the process is far more involved and devastating and think twice about this process. As in Elizabeth's case, the nonresolved parental conflict and resulting acrimony began long before court appearances were even being considered by anyone. Continuous exposure of an innocent and unsuspecting child, like Elizabeth, to parental hostilities has an insidious and profound effect on the child's development. Living in a home environment filled with tension, anger, deceit, mistrust, adult self-involvement, and disregard of or inability to care for the child's emotional and psychological needs almost inevitably shapes the form and substance of the child's enduring personality and character structure. The parents are so involved in their bitterness and battles that the needs of the child are disregarded or overlooked, even by well-meaning adults. In many instances roles become reversed and the child is required to parent the other children in the family and sometimes take care of the needs of the adults as well.

One might assume that when the legal divorce is completed and the day-to-day hostilities subside, the child can then return to normal developmental tasks. But roles within the family rarely return to what they were before everything exploded; life has dramatically changed for everyone. And if you are a child of divorce, none of these changes has been initiated or voted upon by you. Loss, confusion, mistrust, and insecurity provide the context within which the child's future development will take place.

The most basic and universal childhood wish is to be loved by one's parents. This primal longing is often frustrated during the lengthy process preceding and extending through the divorce itself. And if after all of this the parents continue their conflict and hostilities and/or the father withdraws from or even disappears from the child's life, the effects of the loss on the child can be pronounced and virtually irreparable. In those situations in which a child was born to a single mother and never knew its father because he was not identified or did not come forward and accept responsibility for his sexual behavior, the effects on the child's development can be equally devastating.

THE DEVASTATING EFFECTS OF DIVORCE ON CHILDREN

Most children of deadbeat dads do not weather well the absence of a parent. Many are born out of wedlock and never have had a parent who assumed the role of father. Others have lost a parent to divorce at such a young age that they have little conscious memory of it. And still others, of course, were lucky enough to have had a two-parent family for some portion of their childhood and to have experienced a divorce only at a later time. Whether a child knows the father or remembers the break-up consciously, the effects of being raised in a single-parent family are generally negative, profound, and lasting. But when fathers evade and shirk their financial responsibilities to their children, the effects can be more than negative; they can be devastating. Divorce is bad enough but when compounded by the poverty, neglect, and rejection of nonsupport, it may reverberate for generations.

THE PROCESS OF DIVORCE

Divorce is typically viewed as a legal event that settles the marital rights and responsibilities of husbands and wives. While the legal proceedings do begin and end in a finite period of time, divorce is actually not a single event but a process that generally extends over a lengthy and indefinite period. It begins considerably before either husband or wife thinks about going to court and often continues for a long time afterward, sometimes up to a point when children are grown and parental interaction on their behalf is no longer necessary. That's for the adults. For the children, the process of divorce affects them beyond even that point and well into their future as adults. They are truly helpless bystanders who are forced to witness the divorce process and who are powerless to alter a course of events that will have a significant impact on them for the rest of their lives. So while the law attempts to end marriage in an orderly and fair manner, courts are just not able to remedy the severely damaging effects of failed marriages, fractured families, and unmet childhood needs that the dissolution leaves in its wake.

The long-term consequences of divorce make it apparent that divorce must be viewed not as a single dramatic event but rather as a chain of events or processes made up of highly disruptive experiences. It usually begins with an initial period of stress and tension that occurs between spouses while they are still attempting to make their marriage work. Thereafter it extends through separation, divorce, and postdivorce changes in lifestyles, relationships, and roles within the fractured family. This transformation may include single-parent families, new partners of the parents (sometimes resulting in remarriage of one or both of them), the evolution of step-families, visitation, child support needs and sometimes even the breakup of a second family. The effects of divorce go on for years, affecting all aspects of child development.

The particular effects of divorce on any individual child are likely to vary with the child's age, level of development, and, to some extent, gender. For example, older children appear to fare better than their younger counterparts, and girls, in general, seem to do better than boys. Likewise, children who are further along in their intellectual and emotional development have a better chance of doing well in spite of the devastating effects of a family breakup.

Parental conflict, both overt and subtle, is generally the major source of the children's distress. In addition, however, the loss of the adult attention and supervision that may inevitably result from the custodial parent having to return to work, a well as the absence of the noncustodial parent, clearly contributes to identifiable childhood distress. And today, yet another factor in the well-being of children is the decline in socioeconomic status that usually accompanies family breakups. If, for example, prior to the divorce, both parents worked outside of the home to make ends meet, the economic effect of the divorce on the family is obvious. If, on the other hand, prior to the divorce, the father was the breadwinner while the mother cared for the children at home, the economic consequences, while not dire, may result in a significant and distressing disruption in lifestyle. When one considers that the woman can usually expect to earn approximately 68 percent of what a man would earn in the same job, and that women generally occupy fewer well-paying jobs to begin with, the impact on the children's quality of life upon the mother's return to work is very clear.

And then what happens when, in addition to the lifestyle changes and financial restructuring precipitated by the divorce, the absent parent, ordered to contribute to the children's well-being by paying child support, fails to do so? It puts at serious risk the economic survival of the remaining family and is also likely to have a major influence on the emotional stability of the children. Deadbeat dads are responsible not only for depriving their children of necessary goods and services but also for the profound and enduring emotional consequences that their delinquency forces upon these children.

THE STAGES OF DIVORCE

The process of divorce can be viewed as having three identifiable stages. The first stage is the period that leads up to the decision to end the marriage. This stage is marked by high levels of stress and conflict within the family. The parents are in the process of emotionally disconnecting from one another. Intense disagreements and fighting alter the rhythms of daily life for the children, who know that something terrible is going on but feel helpless to do anything about it. Parents, so enmeshed in their own stress and pain, have little time or patience for the fears and anxieties of their children. Children learn to withhold and suppress their feelings to the point of keeping the family's crisis secret from others in their community. For example, if they sense that something is wrong and want to talk about it with a parent, they may be told that their perceptions are inaccurate or that they are misinterpreting the situation or distorting what's going on. This leads to children doubting themselves and mistrusting their own abilities to perceive reality accurately. Unable to trust their own intuitions and perceptions, feeling confused about what is true, and not knowing what to believe, these children may become mistrustful of their relationships with others. The predivorce stage lasts on average from three to five years. This is a long time for children to be exposed to high levels of recurrent or persistent stress.

The divorce itself, the legal proceeding, comprises stage two. This one can move very quickly or can be drawn out for years. Either pattern can cause major disruptions for the children, who sit on the sidelines and watch their own lives unravel. When the process is drawn out, exposure to persistent hostility, divisiveness, conflict, and stress is corrosive and, over time, can erode the will and strength of even the most adaptive and determined child. When appearances in court and signing the papers that finalize negotiated agreements happen too quickly, children can be left devastated, stunned, or numb because they have not had the time to process, integrate, and adapt to what has happened.

The final stage of the divorce process is not defined by an end point as are stages one and two, and for the children it often continues, for all intents and purposes, in an open-ended fashion for much of their lives. Here, the aftershocks of the dissolution of the child's family, such as having an absent parent, having the custodial parent return to work, having parents develop new relationships and even new families, etc., requires continuing adjustments by the child. It is during this postdivorce phase that issues related to nonpayment of child support arise. Continued acrimony between the parents keeps a high stress level for children and may force them into new roles for which they are ill-prepared. For example, some children become the caretakers of a parent whom they feel has been wronged. Others feel they must function as mediators or go-betweens for the parents who seek to continue their battles. Yet one of the worst consequences of this process is the withdrawal of the father's investment in the children's financial security and well-being. Fathers who begin to redevelop their own personal and romantic lives have less time and fewer resources to share with their children. This begets a cycle of decreased time and attention given to children, a decreased sense of personal connection, and, subsequently, decreased financial support. The result is that individual children experience a marked deterioration in lifestyle and there is a dramatic increase in the percentage of children who live below the poverty line.

Divorce is most traumatic for the children. For them, time does not heal all wounds. It affects the development of children's personalities, the quality of their relationships, and their ability to work productively and consistent with their potentials. The following trends have been observed relative to how a particular child will be affected by divorce.

THE EFFECTS OF DIVORCE RELATED TO CHILDREN'S AGES

Preschool children, ages one through five, tend to have little conscious memory of the divorce. They are very young when the process begins and understand little of what is taking place. In the absence of conscious memory, these children are most likely to develop fears of being alone, fears of abandonment, clinginess during times of routine separation from the custodial parent (e.g., going to school or child care or even going to bed) and disruption and regression to less mature levels of play (which is their major mode of expression). Restlessness, irritability, nightmares, aggressiveness, and being possessive of adults are often observed as well. Preschoolers, unable to understand divorce, may worry that they did something or wished something that caused their parents to split up. Even worse, some preschoolers come to believe that the divorce occurred because they themselves are unlovable and therefore deserve being unloved. When children, from their formative years on, develop these feelings and attitudes, they wind up with fear as their closest companion. They grow up always burdened by fears of intimacy, abandonment, and rejection. They wrestle with low self-esteem, retreat from assertive self-expression, and worry about their ability to live in a stable and committed relationship. Despite their young age, they are far from immune to what is going on around them, and many are affected in a lasting way.

Elementary school-aged children, ages six through thirteen, are old enough to be well aware of the strife that accompanies the divorce process. Plagued by prolonged fighting and family stress, many children at this level of development experience a sense of relief when the divorce ends the daily conflicts. But children of these ages are undergoing the major transition from home to school and face different developmental issues. When their home base is crumbling, their ability to attend and concentrate on schoolwork is strained. Grades and test scores suffer. Social difficulties and aggressive behaviors are common in the boys. Depression, open sadness, and crying episodes are not at all uncommon in both boys and girls. Behavior may fluctuate between dependence and rebellion, as children are drawn to the culture and demands of peers while still trying to adjust to the restructuring of their home life. Often children resist the new structure (or lack of structure), trying to hold onto the vestiges of previous patterns and routines. Additionally, the developing morality of children of this age demands that blame be placed for bad behavior. As a result, children in this age group often look for a parent to blame for the divorce, and are easily enlisted in siding with one parent against the other. This can lead to alienation from the identified "bad" parent (usually the non-custodial father) and fuels the flames that can ultimately lead to nonsupport. Furthermore, as children in distress rebel and disconnect from the morality of the adult world, they may begin to believe that adults can no longer be trusted and may experiment with lying, stealing, deception, and other antisocial behavior. For other children, this type of disruptive acting-out behavior is their attempt to focus attention on themselves as a way of rallying the family. These children harbor fantasies of getting their parents back together and become troublesome or actually get into trouble in the hope that their parents will stop fighting between themselves and come to the rescue of the child by reconstructing the family as it once was.

Adolescents, ages fourteen through nineteen, like elementary school-aged children, are also in the process of moving away from the home and are greatly influenced by their peers. Under the best of circumstances, adolescence is a time of conflict and turbulence, as teenagers struggle with establishing their own identities, a process that naturally involves separation from their family. Those who have endured the process of divorce often feel angry, sad, and betrayed that the adults they have previously idolized have let them down by dissolving the very foundation of their lives: the family and its security. Some report feeling numb as a result of so many years of stress leading up to the event. And, lest they think that the

event has ended the struggle, most soon discover that the conflict
continues with a whole host of new problems. Some adolescents
become overly responsible and "parentified," focusing all their
efforts on maintaining a family atmosphere for their younger
siblings. For children going through adolescence and experiment-
ing with love and sex, the breakup of their parents' relationship at
this time can wield a devastating blow to their ability to develop
intimacy and trust. Many of these children experience intense
anger over what they feel is a betrayal of the trust they had that their
parents would always provide a safe and secure laboratory from
which they could venture and experiment. Instead of being able to
count on comfort from their parents during trying times, they are
the ones who are often called on to comfort their parents. Some
may prematurely detach from the family and drift into multiple
unstable relationships, promiscuity, substance abuse, and other
behaviors that reflect their sense of loss of control. Academic
performance frequently deteriorates and problems with truancy
can occur. Other adolescents may shy away from all relationships,
vowing never to become vulnerable to the pain and disappointment sustained by their parents. Still others may swing to the
opposite extreme by becoming prematurely sexually active, mar-
rying early, getting pregnant, etc. While there is a small proportion
of youngsters for whom the divorce truly provides relief and whose
quality of life subsequently improves, for most there is a continued
negative effect well into their adult lives.

THE ENDURING EFFECTS OF DIVORCE ON GROWN CHILDREN

   In all of the age groups, boys appear to fare consistently worse
than girls as they proceed through the postdivorce stage. Despite
this, as they emerge into adulthood, both males and females share
a number of issues characteristic of grown children of divorce. The
most common traits developed when they were children needing
to deal with the trauma of the family breakup.
   Divorce interrupts normal development. Children's attitudes

and behavior by necessity get redirected. They are forced to develop attitudes and adjust their behaviors to help them cope. These very coping behaviors become so deeply ingrained that they endure despite the fact that they may no longer be useful and only make the lives of these children, now adults, unhappy. The following are some examples of the enduring problems that children of divorce often suffer. Some may experience all of them; others may suffer the consequences of only a few. It is unlikely that any child will escape unscathed.

One common problem experienced by these adults is a burdensome sense of responsibility. When their parents were self-absorbed and unavailable, sometimes physically as well as emotionally, the children learned to take responsibility for the care of themselves, often their siblings, and sometimes even their parents. In order to restore some semblance of normality to the shattered family, some children will try to be helpful by taking care of the home and other family members. But in so doing they must deny themselves and suppress their desire to have their own needs met. If they harbored the illusion that they were in some way the cause of the family's problems, they might also believe that if they tried hard enough they could "fix" things. These children were forced to grow up quickly, to be serious, and to give up their natural playfulness and curiosity. As an adult, this type of person exhibits stunted emotional development, and has the emotional maturity of a young child. Poor self-esteem results from feeling helpless in not having been able to solve the parents' problems. These children also have an immature sense of personal identity since they spent most of their time trying to meet the needs of others and never finding out who they themselves really are.

The second common characteristic of adult children of divorce is their need to exercise control over their surroundings, including other people. Having grown up in homes that were either out of control or rigidly overcontrolled and where no amount of effort or accommodation on their part could change what was happening, these children grow up to be adults with a need to control everything around them. They seek structure and clarity in their adult lives as they struggle to deal with the lingering effects of their childhood chaos and confusion. Some may find comfort through membership in rigidly defined organizations and institutions; the certainty, predictability, and stability they offer seem to address an unmet childhood need or hold out the promise of healing a wound. But when the same need for certainty, stability, and control is demanded by them from their personal relationships, the consequences can be, and often are, disastrous. These struggling children of divorce erroneously believe that through the exercise of control they can either mend what is broken or even prevent current events from taking a wrong turn and getting out of hand. They labor under the unfounded belief that they alone know how things should be done and what is good for other people. Thinking that this is the way to get a loved one to stay and not abandon them, which is their goal, it more often than not leads to a recreation of their childhood pain and frustration. For the adult children of divorce the cycle of hurt, rejection, and abandonment is often repeated in their failed adult relationships.

While the most prevalent characteristic of adults who were children of divorce is their need to take responsibility for others and to control the situations and people around them, a number of other features are also observed. Many have a dread of conflict. Having grown up with undue amounts of conflict laden with hostility, as adults they fear conflict and desperately try to avoid it. Others express their own anger in subtle, covert, and destructive ways, such as being noncommunicative, emotionally disconnected, or by invalidating the other person's perceptions and dismissing their thoughts and feelings as unfounded. They can also behave in ways that are designed to inflict hurt, such as using humiliation, making others feel stupid or incompetent, or perhaps even suggesting that they are unstable. Still others use conflict manipulatively. By controlling the level of tension, they themselves are able to "feel" something rather than remain in a state of emotional anesthesia. This can develop into a distorted sense of closeness and intimacy by raising the "feeling" level through conflict. Overcoming emotional inertia this way may be painful, but at least they have a feeling of being alive.

Still another common characteristic among children of divorce is their difficulty establishing personal boundaries. These individuals may have been used by their parents as the place to download their emotional garbage, or as a conduit though which the parents communicated to one another, or as spies, or in some other way that inappropriately pulled them into their parents' drama. Not being able to fend off these destructive behaviors when they were children, as adults they often find situations that recreate their familiar childhood patterns; they perpetuate being used by someone else. This is a common characteristic of individuals who exhibit a sense of helplessness. As straws in the wind of their parents' stormy marriage, nothing they did helped calm the turbulence or kept the family together. As adults, these individuals exhibit serious deficits in communication and social skills. They are frequently confounded by what most people would consider to be ordinary situations. They are confused by simple interpersonal events and have difficulty crafting appropriate responses. More complex intimate relationships pose enormous challenges. Mired in the realities of divorce, with so little innate understanding of how normal families and relationships work, they look to fantasy portrayals, such as television and movies, for ways to model their reactions. Their standards are unrealistic and unobtainable. Consequently, these individuals have circumscribed and rigid ways of viewing others and distorted expectations about intimate relationships. This, of course, affects how they actually relate, and operating from fantasy leads them down the very path that they wanted to avoid. It is no coincidence that so many children of divorce wind up in a divorce situation themselves as adults.

Many of the foregoing issues—feeling inappropriately responsible, needing to exercise control, lacking in communication and social skills, and even experiencing oneself as helpless—are associated with the next major issue that many children of divorce struggle with: the fear of being abandoned. During the process of divorce, parents are typically preoccupied with their own needs and have little time or energy for the children. Even prior to the actual divorce, fathers often leave the home, requiring mothers to suddenly become responsible for the economic survival of the family. At this time the children's lifestyles are also likely to undergo dramatic changes: they may be left more on their own; with the absence of adult supervision, daily routines change or disappear; and money for necessities as well as luxuries is likely to be in much shorter supply. There may be less emotional nurturance or involvement in practical matters from stressed and demoralized parents. As these children enter adult life, they anticipate and fear further abandonment. Some adopt coping strategies that result in leaving their partners before their partners leave them. This makes them feel in control, but is certainly not a formula for successful interpersonal intimacy and stability. Others may try to smother their partners with what they think they want, thus trying to ensure that they will not walk out. Even though it may appear that the person is being showered with kindness and generosity, it is in fact a form of oppression, and it is not unusual for the person to react to being oppressed by leaving the relationship. Whatever coping strategy these children of divorce adopt, when it is carried into their adult life it usually leads to dysfunction.

Finally, divorce often results in constant worry about economic security, not only for custodial mothers but for the children as well. Divorce almost always brings a decline in the standard of living for the custodial parent and her family. Estimates of lowered income range from 30 percent to 73 percent for mothers and children, while fathers may actually experience a 10 percent to 40 percent gain. This reality probably results from the lower earning potential of most women and the fact that many divorced mothers either never remarry or do so only after many years of trying to make ends meet as a single parent. For the children who grew up feeling this constant economic strain, this issue is carried with them into adulthood, and economic considerations and anxieties run their lives. Whether they watched their mothers struggle "to keep the wolf from the door" or listened to their father constantly complaining about the burdens of his financial obligations, or perhaps had a father who disappeared altogether, these children develop into adults with a survival mentality. Regardless of what their own life situations bring, they still fear that they will eventually not be able to take care of themselves, and anxiety over economic matters becomes a life-defining issue.

EFFECTS OF CONFLICT AND NONSUPPORT ON CHILD DEVELOPMENT

Not surprisingly, all children of divorce do not necessarily experience their plight in the same way. While the reality of divorce is negative and painful for most people, some divorces lead to positive results. The painful and disruptive aspects of family dissolution can be counterbalanced by enhanced opportunities for growth and development when a dysfunctional family situation is changed. Two major factors determine how well children will ultimately adjust. First is the level of parental conflict that has existed prior to the divorce, and the duration and the degree to which conflict continues after the family is restructured. In positive divorce situations, the parents recognize that in the best interests of the children they must keep their conflict to a minimum, expose the children to as little upset as possible, and find ways to negotiate their differences that are the least disruptive for the children. To be successful, parents must be willing to manage and deal with their own feelings so that they can behave in a way that makes their responsibility to their children a priority. Denial, secrecy, acrimony, blame, and hostility must be avoided or minimized to the greatest extent possible. Honesty, realism, and the frank expression of needs and feelings through open communication are emphasized. In positive divorce situations the needs of the children are acknowledged and respected, allowing them to develop relationships with both parents despite their parents' disagreements and inability to live together.

It is an unfortunate reality that in most divorces this is not the case. Despite good intentions, too often parents are simply not able to put aside their bitterness and hostility toward one another and truly help their children to cope and adjust to the changes taking place. The second major factor is fathers who are unable or unwilling to meet their child support responsibilities. Nonsupport contributes significantly to economic vulnerability, insecurity, and, in many cases, eventually a life in poverty for divorced single-parent families. Such families move around frequently in search of more affordable housing and better paying jobs. This creates great instability for the children as they leave behind friends, family, and other familiar support systems. Changing schools inhibits academic achievement and social bonding. Mothers, when at home, are often highly stressed, being fatigued from work and trying to manage job, home and children. Furthermore, the mothers are lonely, since their demanding work and family responsibilities leave their personal adult needs unmet. Personal frustrations coupled with constant worry about needing money to pay the bills result in depleted emotional resources in addition to the mother's already scarce financial supplies. Few reserves are left over for the children.

In addition to creating financial hardship and deprivation for the children, there are other effects of the nonpayment of child support. It clearly perpetuates parental conflict, which is the primary cause of poor adjustment of many children. When support is not paid, the third (postdivorce) stage is extended almost indefinitely. It can feel to both mother and child as though the process will never end because the hurt, disappointment, and anger never go away. If the parents need to have continued contact, for example when the nonsupporting ex-spouse continues to have visitation, the conflict is likely to be not only intense but also overt. The war between the parents rages on and the children must constantly deal with their confusion and fear as they duck verbal bullets and negotiate the minefield of explosive emotions.

In fact, in some families the hostilities that may have been acted out covertly before the divorce actually escalate after it has occurred. Children are drawn into taking sides and urged to denounce one parent in favor of the other. Some children are even required to bridge the communication gap between their warring parents, carrying messages regarding a variety of unpleasant topics and negotiations, including messages concerning child support payments. They may begin to feel helpless and isolated, unloved and unlovable. Some fantasize about their parents reuniting, while others contemplate running away from home. Children exposed to this kind of continued traumatic conflict act out more aggression, depression, and delinquent behavior.

Divorce transforms, and can severely damage, the father-child relationship (assuming custody remains with the mother). Even when contact is regular and support is paid, the relationship is never the same as it was before the divorce. Often the father stops behaving like a parent, instead adopting the role of "weekend Santa"—planning trips, going to special events, and showering the children with gifts. The custodial parent, the mother, usually without the time and resources to provide these things, may be resentful or envious of the father's new role. This can cause the children, when they return home, to be secretive or embarrassed and shamed at having to reveal where they have been and what gifts they received. The fun and games with father turn into a veil of guilt with mother. Some children feel that they are living two lives and can't be themselves with either parent.

Finally, even more destructive to children is the increasing tendency for fathers to disappear altogether. The less a father sees his child, the more likely he is to withhold support payments. The more he withholds child support, the less likely he is to reestablish contact. And the more he withdraws, the less likely it becomes that the custodial parent can maintain the positive home environment and attitude conducive to restoring healthy child development. Today we are experiencing a tragedy of epidemic proportions: fathers failing to provide financial support for their children, allowing their children to experience deprivation, even poverty, and thereby altering the course not only of their economic well-being but also their academic, social, and emotional development. And the problem does not stop with the current generation of injured children.

3

The Effect of Fault and No-Fault Divorce Laws on Child Support

INTRODUCTION

It is difficult to imagine that only a generation ago couples seeking to obtain a divorce had to have a legally recognized ground for getting divorced. Each state had developed a statute that set forth the specific grounds that would be permitted in that state. Although there was some variation, typical fault grounds included:

• adultery (sexual intercourse by a married person with anyone other than one's own spouse);
• mental or physical cruelty (including severe physical or emotional abuse but not quarrelsomeness, extravagance, laziness, undue strictness with children, lack of companionship, or callous indifference);
• intoxication (habitual drunkenness) as defined by state law;
• nonsupport (husband's failure to provide suitable maintenance for his wife or family, assuming financial ability);
• impotency (inability to perform sexually, as defined by an individual state law);
• imprisonment (confinement in a state or federal facility for at least a certain period of time designated by state law, usually five

or more years);
• insanity (as legally defined by state law, whether or not confined
to an institution).

Although either party to a marriage could initiate a divorce
action, in reality the large majority of those seeking fault-based
divorces were men. The reasons for this were probably many, but
two, in particular, are often cited. First, men were less stigmatized
for being divorced, and many quickly remarried anyway. Second,
and perhaps more significant, more married men could "afford" to
get divorced while most married women, with little earned income
and often children to be cared for, did not have the luxury of being
unhappy in their marriages and seeking fulfillment elsewhere. Of
course, in extreme cases some women were compelled to leave a
marriage, and some did. But in most cases it was the men who
sought to be divorced, and often a suitable ground had to be
fabricated.

Because of the nature of the fault system of divorce, a wife
typically had substantial leverage over a husband seeking divorce
because he often needed her cooperation to try to demonstrate the
presence of fault grounds in order to obtain his divorce. Assuming
that the wife was not guilty of a genuine fault ground, she would
use her leverage to coerce a desirable financial settlement in the
divorce proceeding. Child custody was rarely an issue since
everyone assumed, in the usual case, that the mother would retain
custody. At the same time, however, she also had a greater need
for support for herself and the children. Thus the wife might offer
to cooperate with a consent decree if her husband was willing to
meet certain financial conditions. This meant that she would not
contest that there were statutory grounds for the divorce, but rather
consent that they were, in fact, present. In essence, the man would
buy his wife's agreement to the divorce by offering her an adequate
economic package.

Tom was having an adulterous affair with Sheri, who
was pressuring him to divorce his wife and marry her.

Tom, in fact, wanted to marry Sheri, but his wife,
Marla, refused to give him a divorce. At the time, no-
fault divorce was not available. After repeated discus-
sions with Marla, she finally agreed to seek a divorce
on grounds of Tom's adultery. In return, Tom agreed
that Marla would retain custody of their three children
and that he would support the children through age
eighteen and Marla indefinitely, except if she remarried.

The practical consequence of fault-based divorce was that it
provided the wife with an important bargaining chip when nego-
tiating for economic security for herself and her children.

DEVELOPMENT OF NO-FAULT LAWS

In 1970, California became the first state in the country to adopt
a no-fault-based ground for divorce. Since that time, virtually
every other state has passed some form of no-fault legislation.
Now commonly known as no-fault divorce, any married person
seeking a divorce can file such a petition with or without the
consent of a spouse. The petition alleges, in essence, that there has
been an "irretrievable breakdown" of the marriage and that a
divorce is sought on that basis. The traditional "fault" grounds
may or may not be present, and when the case is heard both parties
have an opportunity to complain of the misdeeds of the other.
    The no-fault system has developed as a part of a significant
divorce-law reform whose purpose was to end the charade of
perjured testimony and falsified evidence that permitted consent
decrees under the fault system. In practice, no-fault has had a
significant negative economic impact on the women and children
of divorce. When a husband who wants to end his marriage can
simply file a petition alleging that the marriage is irretrievably
damaged, he leaves his wife without a defense to such an allegation
and without a bargaining tool to provide for herself and her
children.

Steve sought a divorce from his wife, Ginny, when he
met Carla, another woman whom he wanted to marry.
Ginny was a homemaker and cared for their two
children, ages seven and nine. Steve sought a no-fault
divorce on grounds that there was an "irretrievable
breakdown" of his marriage to Ginny. Ginny dis-
agreed and wanted to try marriage counseling, but
Steve declined. Ginny didn't even want to participate
in the divorce proceeding, but she had to do so to assert
her custody rights and to get support for herself and
her children. When she was unable to reach an agreement with Steve, the court awarded custody to Ginny,
along with a modest amount of child support and
three years of alimony. Ginny was forced to give up
her life as a full-time homemaker and mother in order
to return to work. The court paid little attention to the
reasons for the divorce.

Although initially hailed as a rational and responsive measure to
an issue that substantially affected the lives of many, no-fault
divorce resulted in many unanticipated consequences, primarily
for children and those women whose occupation was that of a
homemaker. In fact, the fallout of no-fault divorce has been so
disastrous for women and children that in many cases it has
severely reduced or totally eliminated their ability to obtain the
financial security customarily granted to them.

Another major consequence of the reform of the divorce laws has
been that child custody practices have changed. In earlier days,
child custody was almost automatically awarded to the mother
unless she was deemed unfit. This favored stay-at-home mothers
whose "occupation" was to raise their children. The mothers and
children were generally assured of a support award, primarily
because mothers were the primary caretakers, and maternal custody resulted in continuity of child care.

Today women who seek to stay at home and be supported by their ex-husbands face an uphill battle. First, economic circumstances often make it prohibitive, because many divorced fathers cannot even support themselves, let alone pay adequate child support and support two households without a second income. The consequence has been that mothers must return to the work force, at least on a part-time basis. Second, many men are now contesting the assumption that women should automatically become the sole custodians of children. Alternative arrangements, such as joint child custody (discussed in chapter 6), challenge the need for mothers to be full-time homemakers, even if their ex-husbands can afford to maintain them in that role.

> Cindy had been at home with her three children, now ages thirteen through seventeen, since their births. Her husband, Paul, maintained the support of the family. When Paul filed for a no-fault divorce, he also sought custody of their children. The couple ended up with joint custody and both parents were expected to contribute to the children's support. Paul did pay some alimony, but his income was simply inadequate to support himself and Cindy separately as well as contribute to the support of the children. The standard of living for Cindy and the children went down considerably, even though Cindy went to work.

A third factor in the difficulty women have in continuing as homemakers following divorce is their ex-husbands' resentment. Women have almost always been awarded custody of their children under both the fault and no-fault based systems of divorce because the "fault" or "innocence" of a party still has a bearing on child custody. Courts make custody decisions on the basis of what is best for the children. Any allegations against either party of cruelty, intoxication, desertion, or any of the other legal grounds will likely affect the court's award of child custody. In many cases, the wife is the "innocent" party, at least with respect to the legal grounds that courts recognize. (Men perpetrate most of the physical and/or psychological abuse; men more often desert a family, etc.) As a result, women have always had an advantage in retaining child custody, but more often today, men resent paying support without a fair opportuntity to assert custodial rights.

NO-FAULT IN PRACTICE

The mechanics of no-fault law are that either spouse is entitled to assert that irreconcilable differences have caused an irretrievable breakdown of the marriage. Exactly what constitutes an irretrievable breakdown under a particular no-fault statute is unclear, but generally one or both parties will allege serious marital discord that makes it impossible to continue to function as husband and wife. In most states a no-fault divorce can be granted even if one party does not agree to it, or indeed, if only one party shows up at the hearing. The implication is that no fault is ascribed to either party, i.e., the breakdown of the marriage was not precipitated by cruelty on the part of either partner nor did other fault grounds exist. In practice, the designation of the grounds for a divorce is often negotiated by the parties. It is not uncommon, for example, for one partner to file for divorce based upon a fault grounds and ultimately reach a settlement of the financial issues and change the petition for divorce to a no-fault proceeding.

Betsy filed a petition for divorce against her husband, Ken, alleging cruelty and desertion. Ken had moved out of the marital home after nearly nine years of marriage. Initially, he contested custody and sought a substantial share of the marital assets. Eventually, however, they were able to work out a settlement including child custody, support, and division of the marital assets. When the agreement was reached, they filed a joint petition for a no-fault divorce, which allowed the hearing to proceed more quickly.

The apparent purpose of the no-fault laws was not to require people to somehow justify their desire to get divorced but only to require that they provide for the dependents of the marriage.

Traditional divorce laws based upon fault required the courts by statute to make dispositions of property as well as awards of child custody and support on the basis of what they deemed just and fair under the circumstances. Courts would use their discretion in allowing evidence of fault, because being found guilty or innocent in a divorce action had important consequences for alimony, property division, and child custody. In fact, under traditional law, the purpose of alimony was to financially "reward" an innocent spouse and to "punish" a guilty one. In practice, a wife found guilty of adultery might not be awarded alimony, while a husband found guilty of adultery might be ordered to pay excessive punitive alimony to his ex-wife. The same would be true for desertion. Since, historically, most cases involved a husband abandoning his wife, the wife, as the innocent spouse, would receive a larger alimony award if her husband was at fault.

More than twenty years after the first no-fault laws went into effect, it appears that no-fault reform, instead of resulting in economic equality between spouses, has instead yielded economic detriment to women, sometimes with a windfall to men. No-fault has escalated the incidence of female heads of household and has substantially lowered the economic resources available to divorced women and their children. In fact, women and children now seem to get much fewer assets and support under no-fault laws as compared with settlements under the fault systems, although even under the fault regime, a woman's economic status ended up substantially lower than that of her husband.

Specifically, under no-fault, alimony is granted less frequently; it is awarded in smaller amounts and for shorter duration; child support awards are smaller and not necessarily always granted (depending upon custody); property settlements awarded to the wife have decreased; and, at the same time, the percentage of family debt awarded to the wife has increased.

A study conducted by the U.S. Census Bureau and completed in late 1992 reported that a high percentage of women and children fall below the poverty line after a divorce. The statistics indicate that the average income of newly formed single-parent families dropped by 37 percent within four months of the breakup of a family. At the same time, dependency upon the welfare system doubled. In fact, divorce was found to be the leading cause of poverty among women and children. The Census Bureau also reported in the same study that 25 percent of absent fathers make no child support payments at all and another 25 percent make only partial payments.

Under traditional fault rules, courts usually awarded alimony to an "innocent" spouse for life. Fault-based awards would generally be increased periodically to reflect the increased cost of living and, if necessary, would be modified if the original award was insufficient to support the dependents.

Under no-fault law, the court's greatest emphasis is on two factors: (1) the wife's employability, and (2) the duration of the marriage. Temporary ("transitional" or "rehabilitative") alimony has become much more common than permanent alimony. This type of award is frequently granted to wives (usually) who may have left the work force or a training program to assume the responsibilities of being a married woman and mother. With few or outdated skills, she is given a limited period of time and support to "rehabilitate" herself and re-enter the work force. Under the no-fault system, modifications and increases in support are the exception. Economic consequences for women of divorce have become so dire largely as a result of these important changes.

Karen quit college in order to marry Ted and move to Chicago, where he had a position as an accountant. They had one child who was eight years old at the time the couple separated. Karen, age twenty-nine, had few marketable skills and had not worked outside of the home since the marriage. The court awarded her custody of the child and three years of "transitional" alimony for the stated purpose of allowing Karen to return to college and finish her degree. After that, Ted was ordered to pay child support only and in an amount that provided for only a portion of the child's actual needs.

Today transitional awards are common and are intended primarily to enable a dependent spouse to get back on her feet and obtain the education or training necessary to return her to the work place. In reality, that purpose is rarely accomplished, particularly in the relatively short period of time that is allocated.

Under the no-fault divorce laws, the average awards are smaller. In part, this may be the result of the altered bargaining position of women in no-fault divorce situations, but it is also likely that many judges presume that many women will, in fact, secure suitable employment after the divorce; the awards are set accordingly. Here again, in reality more often than not the courts underestimate the difficulty that a homemaker faces in finding a job that will make her self-sufficient.

In many instances, alimony is virtually unheard of for women who are divorced in the early years of marriage (i.e., short-term marriages) under the current no-fault laws. Unless a woman has children at home and her husband is willing and able to maintain her as a primary caretaker, even women with children (except, perhaps, very young ones) will usually be expected to be self-supporting within a short period of time. Professional women in particular are rarely awarded alimony, even if they choose to be at home with the children and their husbands can afford to support them. The consequence is that motherhood is no longer a secure occupation, even in a household that can afford it, and stay-at-home mothers have no guarantee that they will continue to be supported in that role after a divorce.

Andrea is a real estate broker; her husband, Ron, is an engineer. They had been married for six years and had two young children when they separated. Andrea was working only occasionally and expected to continue in that capacity, at least until the children were in

school. To her surprise, however, she was awarded
only a small amount of alimony and only for two
years. Ron actually had a substantial income and
could have afforded to keep Andrea at home. After the
divorce, Andrea and the children barely got by on the
support that Ron was ordered to pay. Ron, on the
other hand, pursued his life style undeterred, paying
a modest amount of support and assuming little of the
responsibility for extraordinary expenses, such as home
repair, medical bills, and child care.

REALITIES OF TODAY'S DIVORCE LEGISLATION

Women and children of divorce suffer economically for a
number of intangible reasons as well. In order for a woman to get
a decent financial settlement, she has to have substantial knowledge of the family's financial picture. A woman who is ignorant
about her husband's assets, income, investments, and expenses
risks being taken advantage of by self-interested husbands and
unscrupulous divorce lawyers. At the same time, many women are
unrealistic about their own needs, particularly if they have not
participated in paying bills and balancing the accounts. Their own
lawyers, who should assist them and provide guidance based on
experience with divorce situations, do not always take the time and
pay attention to a particular client's individual circumstances.

Another "intangible" factor is that people in divorce are too often
so emotionally shattered that they simply do not have the wherewithal to pursue the financial aspects of the divorce with the
necessary vigor to protect themselves and their children. More
often than not, it is the women who are in this position. Sometimes,
particularly in recent years, a husband will contest child custody,
primarily to coerce a better financial settlement. In other cases
women do not understand the economic consequences of divorce
until it is too late. And in still other cases, one party or the other
(but mostly the woman) is willing to accept a smaller than adequate
award simply to avoid the fight, to avoid going to court, to maintain

a better relationship with the soon-to-be ex-spouse, or to assuage a guilty conscience resulting from walking away from a marriage and family. Too often it is the children who pay the price for the parent's right to exit peacefully.

Finally, as already mentioned, in an increasing number of cases there is simply not enough income to go around and support two households. Even when previously unemployed wives return to work, once child care costs are factored in, the net result is little more money than if they weren't working. In a time of high unemployment, overburdened social programs, frequent divorces, and an alarming federal deficit, it is of little surprise that there is a scurry to find solutions.

So how have the no-fault divorce laws affected the children of divorce? When their parents separate, they are no longer guaranteed continuity of child care, even if their primary caretaker is willing to stay at home and the family has the means. They are still likely to reside primarily with their mother, although fathers, who no longer have to negotiate their way through the divorce, may assert greater rights of custody and companionship. Children's standards of living have dropped, substantially in fact, to the extent that their household income is likely to be approximately one-third of its predivorce level. Finally, as the rate of divorce has climbed, more children have found themselves living in single-parent households, i.e., without the continuity and balance of having two parents at home.

4

When Paternity Is Contested . . .

CASE STUDY: KRISTEN

When I got pregnant with my daughter Kim, Jeff and I had been having marital problems. In fact, Jeff had moved out of the house for awhile and I had started seeing Paul. I always thought that somehow or other Jeff and I would work it out, so I never thought of being with Paul as having a future. We talked about being together and did have sex, but when I found out about the pregnancy I couldn't imagine how it could have happened. Jeff and I had only been together once in the previous three months and I was pretty sure that I couldn't get pregnant then. And Paul—he was always so careful. We never took a chance that I might get pregnant.

I was totally confused about Jeff and Paul and the prospect of having a child. I had thought a lot about what it might be like to be a parent, and in many ways the reality of pregnancy was really exciting for me. On the other hand my marriage to Jeff was on the rocks, and Paul was just a casual affair. I knew that I really needed to get my life straightened out before I could bring a child into the world. But now I was pregnant and without even considering that the pregnancy might be terminated, I knew this child was going to be born.

When Jeff found out about the pregnancy, he was livid. He had suspected that I was seeing someone else but I always told him that it wasn't serious, which, in fact, it wasn't. Jeff insisted that the child wasn't his and it was hard for me, too, to believe that it was. When I told Paul about the pregnancy, his reaction surprised me even more. He was certain that the child wasn't his, and accused me of betraying him and seeing Jeff on the side. It didn't help when I reminded him that I was married to Jeff—Paul considered it confirmation that Jeff and I were still together, even though Jeff was angry and couldn't care less about me and the pregnancy.

I used every penny I had to pay for the doctor and the hospital bills, and the eight weeks of maternity leave that I got from my job didn't include any salary. I was barely scraping by with no help from Jeff. Surprisingly, though, Paul, who was really distant during the pregnancy, seemed really to take an interest in Kim. We both knew, of course, that she might be his and he seemed to delight in the prospect of fatherhood, but he was also reserved, and you could see him wondering every time he saw Kim. At one point I suggested one of those DNA paternity tests but he said they weren't conclusive, particularly if Jeff didn't get tested, too. I knew that Jeff wouldn't agree so I didn't push it.

As the end of my maternity leave came close and I knew that I had to go back to work, I began to get scared. I couldn't risk losing my job and I couldn't afford not to work anyway. I was getting nothing from Jeff and only an occasional bag of groceries from Paul. He was clear about not wanting to commit to Kim unless he was sure that she was his. As time went on and the expenses of the baby mounted, I knew that I had to find out who Kim's father was and make him help with the finances.

My girlfriend was dating a man who worked in a law firm, and he offered to help me in going to court to force Jeff and Paul to be tested for paternity. It actually wasn't all that difficult in the beginning, but I was so scared about going to court. At one point the judge asked me who I thought Kim's father was, and I just sat there like a dummy, not knowing what to say. I made it through, though, and the judge ordered that Jeff and Paul both be tested. I had mixed feelings about finding out who the father was; I wasn't prepared to be tied to either of these men, but I needed the financial help and there were times that I needed help with the baby, too.

Both Jeff and Paul were relatively civilized about doing the tests. They both agreed to pay for their own, which was great since I had no money to pay for them. I could feel the hesitation on the part of both of them, particularly Jeff, probably because he wasn't so sure that Kim wasn't his. I didn't know how he would react if we found that she really was. He was making plans to get divorced, which was fine with me. It felt really strange, though, to be finding out after all of these months about Kim's father. She barely knew either Jeff or Paul and I wasn't sure that I was willing to share her with either of them. That wasn't fair to Kim, though, and I knew that someday she'd want to know. I was pretty confused, wasn't I?

Jeff's test came back quickly and it was negative. I think that I felt relieved, but I was surprised at Jeff's reaction that seemed so matter-of-fact. He didn't want me; he didn't want my child; and yet there was still a part of him that seemed a little disappointed that the test was negative. His comments to me were slow and controlled, and I'm sure I detected a hint of sadness about the whole matter.

I told Paul as soon as Jeff's results were in and he was really excited. His results hadn't even come back yet but he seemed like a different man. Apparently all those months of thinking seriously about fatherhood and watching Kim grow really touched off a strong feeling in him to be a part of us. Kim was just fabulous and it was tough not to adore her. In fact, Paul immediately started making plans for all of us, which scared me because I wasn't sure that I was ready to make another commitment. Jeff and I weren't even divorced yet.

Paul's tests came back a few weeks later and indicated there was a 98.34 percent probability that he was Kim's father. I have no idea how the tests work and why it wasn't just "positive" or "negative" like Jeff's was. One of the technicians explained that it was a lot

easier to tell who isn't the father than who is. Anyway, that was all
Paul needed to hear. He came around much more often, he started
paying for things for Kim and me, and he even offered to help me
out with my divorce from Jeff.

After the test results and Paul's obvious interest in Kim, I decided
not to go back to court to pursue the paternity suit. But to my
surprise, the court followed up and wanted to issue a final dispo-
sition. And even though I told them that Paul and I were planning
to get married, the court still wanted the paternity proceeding
finished so that there was some formal record of it. With Jeff ruled
out, the hearing was pretty straightforward and I didn't even need
a lawyer to get through it.

DISCUSSION OF KRISTEN'S CASE

In many jurisdictions, a child born to a married woman is
"presumed" to be a child of the marriage. This means that the
husband is presumed to be the father (with all of the attendant rights
and responsibilities) unless he is permitted—and able—to demonstrate that he is *not* the father. If the couple subsequently
divorces—even if the partners were separated at the time of
conception—the husband remains obligated for the support of the
child.

Sometimes a man will assume the paternity of a child born to his
wife and "hold himself out" as the child's father, even if he knows
himself not to be the father or if his paternity is uncertain. If there
is a subsequent divorce, he may raise the question of paternity for
the first time in the divorce proceeding. In most cases, a man who
assumes paternity (either by signing the birth certificate or giving
the appearance to the community that he is the child's father)
cannot later deny that he is the child's father. This is often true even
if he learns for the first time during the divorce proceeding that he
is not or may not be the father of the children.

In past years, an unmarried mother would often look to AFDC for
support of her child(ren) without attempting to identify and pursue
the child's father for support. Today, however, all jurisdictions are

obligated to assist single mothers in taking an active role in establishing paternity; they risk losing benefits if they refuse to participate. It is not unusual, for example, for a hospital with an active maternity ward to offer assistance with establishing paternity to an unmarried woman who does not identify the father of her child.

It is estimated today that nearly 30 percent of the births in the United States are to unmarried women. In 1993 alone, almost 3.5 million children who were eligible for child support required assistance with establishing paternity. That year, more than half a million paternities were established.

PATERNITY LAWS

In recent years, an ever-increasing number of children have been born without a father who acknowledges his fatherhood. The number of out-of-wedlock births has skyrocketed, and there has also been a dramatic increase in the number of cases involving husbands or wives who claim that a child conceived within a marriage was fathered by another man. One of the many consequences of this is that such children do not obtain their legal right of the care and support of two parents.

In earlier years, when the social welfare system borne by the state and federal governments was not as overburdened as it is today and when these cases were fewer in number, many families without fathers were supported by Aid to Families with Dependent Children (AFDC). Attempts were made to establish paternity—i.e., to identify the father of the child—but few were successful. One of the major reasons for this was that the available biological tests were not very sophisticated. Their primary ability was to establish that a "putative" father—a man claiming or claimed to be the father—was *not,* in fact, the father. The method involved blood tests of the mother, father, and child. If the child had a blood type that could not have been inherited from that father, paternity was denied. If the child had the blood type of the mother or of neither parent, the test was unable to assist in establishing paternity.

Two things have happened in recent years to change this scenario. First, the number of so-called deadbeat dads has escalated to a point that the AFDC and other public programs can no longer support all of their children. Second, the technology available to establish paternity with a high degree of certainty is now available through both blood and so-called genetic marker tests. Additionally, both federal and state governments have renewed their commitments to finding absent fathers, establishing their paternity, and pursuing them to support their children. All states are now required to provide assistance for both AFDC and non-AFDC recipients in finding and testing these reluctant dads.

Paternity laws differ from state to state, but the general rule is that a man is presumed (that is, the law says he is unless he can prove otherwise) to be the father of a child under one or more of the following circumstances:

• he was married to the mother at the time of the child's birth or conception;
• he married or attempted to lawfully marry the mother at the time of the child's birth or conception, but the marriage was annulled or declared invalid (e.g., one parent was not yet legally divorced from a former spouse);
• he voluntarily assumed custody of the child (with or without the mother) and held the child out to the public as belonging to him;
• under state law, he voluntarily acknowledged paternity or parental responsibility, without objection of the mother;
• with the consent of the mother, his name appears on the birth certificate of the child.

Historically, a determination of paternity of an unmarried man was considered to be a criminal proceeding that would be brought under a state law that made "desertion" of a child (or a wife) a criminal offense. Many states had adopted some form of a popular Uniform Desertion and Nonsupport Act, making it part of their state law that a man must support his child. The penalties under such laws included both fines and imprisonment. In later years, some of the laws became unenforceable because they were found to be unconstitutional (primarily because fathers but not mothers could be prosecuted under the law). The result was that the proceedings to establish paternity became quasi-criminal or civil matters, to be handled by family courts rather than criminal courts.

Today the primary purpose of paternity laws is to give to children born out of wedlock the same rights and privileges as those who are born within wedlock. This means that children are entitled to the support, if not the companionship, of both parents. The duty of support extends until the child is eighteen years old (or, in some states, twenty-one, if he or she is still dependent) unless the child is emancipated (e.g., the child gets married or joins the military service). In a number of cases, children have even been held entitled to a college education if the parent(s) are able to afford it.

ESTABLISHING PATERNITY

Paternity can be established in a number of ways. The first is by agreement of the parties that a particular man is the father of the child in question. The procedures vary by state, but if the parents are unmarried, they can register their voluntary acknowledgment of paternity in the appropriate court or on the birth certificate of the child. If the mother was married to another man at the time of the conception or birth of the child, both her husband and the putative or alleged father, as well as the mother, may be required to agree voluntarily to paternity. Some states, but not others, require the court to approve the voluntary acknowledgment in what is usually a routine procedure. Once it is approved, it cannot be challenged at a later time.

> Lisa and Jeff were separated when Lisa became pregnant. Although no plans had been made to divorce at the time, it was clear that Jeff would object to legal responsibility for the new child. When the child was born, Lisa's boyfriend, Mark, agreed to assume the paternity of the child, even though Lisa and Jeff were

still married. Mark's name was put on the birth
certificate and Jeff and Mark filed a Voluntary Stipula-
tion of Paternity with the court.

The alternative method of establishing paternity, if the necessary
parties will not agree, is through a lawsuit, usually called a
Complaint for Paternity or similar title. The lawsuit is often filed
by the mother of the child (even if she is a minor) but may,
depending on the state, be filed by other persons, including the
following:

- a man who claims to be the child's father;
- the child;
- the child's next of kin (i.e., a close relative) or legal guardian;
- a representative of the mother (such as a grandmother) if the
mother has died or abandoned the child;
- a state department of social services or similar agency if it has
possession of the child;
- the state department that pays for the support of the child if it
receives public assistance.

Another tricky issue concerning who can file the lawsuit is that,
in some states, a person who alleges that he is the father may not
be entitled to bring a suit for determination of paternity if the
mother is or was married to another man at the time of conception
and/or birth of the child. The law in this area is changing, but only
some states will allow a man to claim that he is the father of a child
born or conceived within another marriage.

The first question that normally arises when a woman considers
bringing a lawsuit to establish the paternity of her child is where to
bring the suit, particularly if the putative father lives in another
state. State laws vary, but the general rule is that the complaint
should be filed in the state and county or district in which the
putative father (defendant) lives or resides. It does not matter that
the mother or even the child lives in another state. In many cases
the state in which they do live will not hear the case if the father is

absent; at the same time the mother (and child) will not be stopped from filing a lawsuit in a state where they do not live. Also, the mother and/or child is not prevented from pursuing a paternity suit if the putative father fails to appear as long as he is given proper notice of the lawsuit and an opportunity to contest it.

In some cases, the woman does not know who the father of the child is but knows of more than one possible candidate. In such an instance, she can sue all putative fathers in the same lawsuit. The court will order, as in any case of contested paternity, that all defendants submit to whatever tests of paternity that the state requires and will use in court. If after testing it is determined that a man could not be the father of the child, he will automatically be dismissed from the case.

> Melissa was single when she became pregnant and gave birth to her son. When she learned of her pregnancy, she believed that any one of three men (Steve, Jerry, or Carl) could have been the father. Each, however, rejected the possibility. After the child was born, all three were required to submit to paternity tests, virtually on the basis of Melissa's word that each had had "sexual access" within the period of time in which she became pregnant. After the testing, Carl was dismissed from the case on the basis that he could not have been the biological father. When the case went to trial, both Steve and Jerry were defendants and the result of each paternity test was admitted. Interestingly, the judge was also entitled to consider which man looked like the boy.

PATERNITY TESTS

The tests available today are substantially more sophisticated than those available only a few years ago. These new tests are known as genetic markers; they examine and match red blood cell antigens, red cell enzymes, serum proteins, human leucocyte antigens (HLA), and whatever other genetic indicators are available and considered reliable. What is becoming available now, for example, are new genetic markets that are being defined by DNA analysis. The technology is rapidly becoming available to be applied to paternity testing.

The simplest test, however, continues to be the blood test, which is often used first for exclusionary purposes. A putative father will be excluded as a possible candidate for paternity if the child has a blood type that is different from its mother and could not have come from him. Genetic markers, however, test a number of genetic materials and are used along with specific information (such as whether the father had sexual access to the mother at or around the probable time of conception). The genetic markers result in a statement of the probability that a particular man could be the father of the child in question. Their current probability of exclusion of paternity is now in the range of 99 percent which means that approximately 99 out of 100 men that are falsely accused of paternity will be deemed to be telling the truth on the basis of the testing. In most states, the tests are sufficiently reliable as a scientific method to be admissible in the courts.

A final method of paternity testing that may be admissible in some courts is the polygraph, or lie detector, test. This evaluation of who is telling the truth is useful when there is a question of whether or not there was sexual access to the mother, which is one factor considered in determining probability of paternity. Either the mother or the father may voluntarily take a polygraph test that addresses the issue of access (i.e., did they have sex), and it is up to the individual state and court to determine whether the result will be admitted into evidence. Generally, the polygraph is admitted in paternity proceedings if (and to the same extent) it is allowed into evidence in other civil matters.

When a paternity case is ultimately given a hearing in court, the rules concerning what procedures will be followed and what evidence will be considered by the court differ not only by state but also from what occurs in the usual civil case. Paternity cases are generally considered to be private matters, and the public is excluded from the hearings. There also is no right to a trial by jury in many states, which means that a judge will hear the case and determine the outcome. In some states, the judge is allowed to consider the resemblance between the child and both its mother and the putative father, even though there is no scientific basis for determining that a relationship exists simply on the basis of appearance. As a practical matter, however, a judge is likely to notice the presence or absence of a strong resemblance, and it is likely to have some influence on his or her decision.

In virtually all cases, the mother will be required to testify about whether the putative father had sexual access to her during the likely time that the child was conceived.

Kim brought a complaint for paternity, alleging that Allen was the father of her illegitimate child. Allen admitted that he had engaged in a sexual relationship with Kim in the past but denied that he had done so within at least two months of the probable time of conception. Both parties were required to answer questions about where they were living, who they dated, and other matters concerning the possibility of sexual contact.

The putative father will also be required to testify, unless he claims his fifth amendment privilege, i.e., he can decline to testify in a court of law (or similar proceeding) if to do so would result in his incriminating himself. In states where adultery is a crime, this might be applicable. In those cases in which the results of the paternity tests are less certain, the judge's assessment of the credibility of the parties is an extremely important consideration. Finally, if the putative father fails to show up at the hearing, a decision can still be made in his absence, and he will be required to abide by it.

LEGAL QUESTIONS CONCERNING PATERNITY

There have been a variety of difficult legal questions that have arisen around the country pertaining to the issue of paternity. One of these concerns what is known as "reverse paternity" cases—those in which biological fathers are asserting their rights of paternity and visitation with a child who was born to a woman while she was married to another man. The rule used to be that a child born to a married couple was presumed to be a product of the marriage. If either the husband or wife was inclined to dispute that presumption, he or she would have to prove that the husband was (1) impotent, (2) sterile, or (3) had no sexual access to his wife at the time of conception.

The courts have generally been reluctant to allow a paternity action without the consent of the husband and wife. But times are changing. In a California case that reached the United States Supreme Court in 1989, a man attempted to establish that he was the biological father of a child born within the wedlock of a married couple. In a split decision, the court held that under the particular circumstances of that case, where there had been no stable relationship between the putative father and the child at the time the paternity proceeding was brought, and because of the absence of a relationship, he was barred from claiming paternity. It is significant that a majority of the justices agreed that under different circumstances, a biological father might have the right to establish paternity.

A more common situation occurs in cases in which husbands or wives will attempt to establish, long after the birth of a child, that a husband, married to the child's mother, was not the biological father of a child born of the marriage. This is usually asserted during a divorce proceeding or even in a subsequent suit for modification of a support award. Either the husband or the wife, or both, may seek to demonstrate that the ex-husband was not the father of the child. In a Michigan case, for example, a man married a woman knowing that she was carrying a child that may or may not have been his. After seven years, in which he held himself out as the father of the child, the court denied him the opportunity to prove that he was not the biological father. In some states, the court would call such a father an "equitable parent," which means that even if he was biologically determined not to be the father, he had assumed that obligation and would be treated as the natural parent. The law varies depending on the state, and the courts must determine on an individual basis whether and when they will allow parents to contest the biological fatherhood of a given individual.

Yet another occurrence is that during paternity proceedings, or at some point thereafter, the parents of the child marry each other. In general, the courts will complete a paternity proceeding that has already been started unless there is a voluntary acknowledgment of paternity, which usually ends the proceeding.

> Richard had been dating Sandy when she announced that she was pregnant. He refused to acknowledge paternity, however, because he knew that Sandy had also been seeing Ted on and off, and Richard wasn't certain that the child was his. Unable to support the child alone, Sandy filed a paternity proceeding against both Richard and Ted when the child was born. After the proceeding was started, Richard and Sandy decided to marry each other. Richard also agreed to acknowledge paternity, even though none of the parties knew who the actual father was.

It is important to the courts that a paternity action, once filed, not be left uncertain even if the parents marry. What concerns the courts is that in the event of a subsequent divorce or support proceeding, they have the paternity question settled so that it need not be reexamined later.

EFFECTS OF PATERNITY RULINGS

So what happens if the court does, in fact, find that a particular man is the father of a child? First, the determination is valid for all purposes and includes having a new birth certificate issued for the child, if necessary. It entitles the child to the financial support of its father as though it had been born within a marriage or had been formally acknowledged by agreement. The laws are intended to provide the same level of support to children born out of wedlock as are available to children born within a marriage. This means that all children are entitled to be supported in accordance with the father's capability until age eighteen or twenty-one, depending upon the state law.

A finding of paternity also means that the father is entitled to child custody or visitation, even if the mother is living with or married to another man. A determination of custody or visitation is always made by the court on the basis of what it considers to be in the best interest of the child. In order for a man who is found to be the father of a child to obtain rights of custody or visitation, he must initiate a separate proceeding (although often in the same court). Except in extreme situations, the court will usually allow at least limited visitation for a man who is ordered to pay support.

Another effect of a paternity proceeding concerns cases in which the mother of the child dies, abandons a child, places it up for adoption, or has the child involuntarily removed from her custody because of abuse, neglect, or inability to care for it. In such a case, a biological father who is unmarried to the mother has a right of custody if he has acknowledged paternity or if it has been established through a paternity proceeding. Unless paternity has already been determined, however, a man who did not previously establish his paternity will probably lose any right to custody.

In the case of adoption, a man who claims to be the biological father may attempt to have his paternity established in order to contest the adoption. Again, laws vary, but in general, before an adoption can take place, both parents or any putative fathers (if there is no acknowledgment of paternity) must be notified. If a man responds and establishes his paternity, he can contest the adoption. Once again, the standard is always the best interests of the child, and there is no automatic right of a biological father to assume custody just because the mother has relinquished her rights. There is, however, some preference for biological parents, and a man who proves his paternity can bring his own petition for adoption.

Yet another effect of paternity proceedings concerns a child's right to inherit from its biological father, whether a trust or will is left. If the father dies intestate, i.e., leaves no will, a child fathered out of wedlock can claim a right to his estate only if his father either voluntarily acknowledged paternity during his lifetime or was determined to be the father during a paternity proceeding. This presents the more difficult question of whether the court can make a determination of paternity after the man has died in order to allow the child to inherit from him. This, too, is an issue of state law, which will determine whether and under what circumstances a child will be allowed to proceed with such a paternity action.

> Peter died without leaving a will. The state law provides that in the absence of a will, each child inherits equally. Peter left three legitimate children, who were born while he was married to their mother. He also left one illegitimate child, Matt, who was born to a woman Peter lived with after he got divorced. Matt's birth certificate contains no indication of fatherhood. However, Matt's mother claims that Peter openly held out Matt as his son.

In those cases in which there is a will, but it refers only to "children" or "issue," courts treat all biological children as equals whether or not they had the benefit of parents being married. This assumes, however, that paternity has been acknowledged or established. Once again, it is up to the individual state to determine whether it will allow a paternity proceeding to be instituted after the putative father has died.

The determination of paternity has proven to be an increasingly important means of securing child support. Many deadbeat dads manage to beat the system because they are not compelled to undergo a formal determination of paternity. But now states have become committed to spending money to purse paternity actions on behalf of all children for whom they are responsible. Once paternity is established, however, collection of support is still a major hurdle.

5

Legal Guidelines for Establishing and Enforcing Child Support Awards

CASE STUDY: BARBARA

Dan and I were divorced six years ago after he had an affair with a woman in his office. I filed for divorce and custody of our two children: Jake, now age fifteen, and Jenny, now thirteen. At one point during our separation Dan made some noise about wanting custody, but we both knew that he didn't have a prayer and I never believed that he was serious about it anyway. My lawyer said this was often used as a bargaining chip and Dan was always willing to bargain.

After much posturing, we managed to reach an agreement that called for custody of the children with me, visitation for Dan, and $100 per child per week of child support. I had worked throughout our marriage, and alimony for me was never even discussed. Well, right from the start collecting child support was a nightmare. If Dan heard that I had a date, the check wouldn't come. If Dan missed his visitation—even when he canceled—the check wouldn't come. If Dan didn't like something that I said, the check wouldn't come. And so on and so on.

Dan eventually remarried and when his new wife became pregnant, he found less and less time for our children. First, extra hours at the office kept him away. Then it was the wedding plans. Then it was his wife's pregnancy... When the visitation dwindled down to an evening or two a month, the children were not surprised. They believed that his new family was more important to him than they were, and Dan did little to change that.

The support payments were no different. At times they would arrive regularly; more often they would be irregular and sporadic. The best weeks were when he seemed to feel guilty about not spending time with our children, but even that never lasted long. Then Dan and his wife had a second child and the support was even less predictable. I know that money was tight for them, and Dan never had a strong sense of responsibility. But what happened next floored even me.

Our son, Jake, broke his leg at basketball practice. The school called me first and I dropped everything and actually made it to the hospital even before the ambulance. I checked him in, providing information on his medical insurance, which Dan carried through his company. It was an excellent plan and would cover virtually all of the expense, which eventually amounted to thousands of dollars because of a multiple compound fracture and some other complications. When the first bill arrived I assumed it to be a hospital error and immediately submitted it to Dan's insurance company. They didn't seem to pay it right away, and in the meantime monthly statements would arrive from the hospital— first informing me that I was ultimately responsible for payment; then requesting, urging, and finally demanding that it be paid. Jake usually got the mail first and he got pretty upset (as did I) when the collection notices came. A couple of times he mentioned it to Dan, but each time he was assured that the processing just took a while.

Five months after the accident, without a word from the insurance company, I decided to take the matter into my own hands. I called Dan's company and even the insurance company itself and was astonished to hear what I was told: the claim had been paid directly to Dan several months earlier—promptly, in fact—and Dan had pocketed the money. And all the while he was telling me—and his own son—that the proverbial check was in the mail.

My outrage at what Dan had done was compounded by my uncertainty about what to tell the children. The relationship that they had with their father was already lukewarm, and I wanted no part in making it worse. Not that I didn't want to get back at Dan. I would be all for that. But I knew that the kids had already been through so much. To tell them now that their father had—in essence—stolen from us and then lied about what he had done was certain to be another blow to the children. They were already feeling that they had been abandoned by Dan and I was afraid that if they were told about this they would feel so hurt that it would be something that they could never forgive.

The reasons for not telling the children about their father's latest charade seemed compelling, but at the same time it was becoming more and more difficult both to contain my own outrage and maintain the illusion that everything was normal. As a practical matter our children were now teenagers and Jake, in particular, was asking regularly about whether the medical insurance was covering his expenses (which were still mounting). So what was I supposed to do, lie to him? And if (or when) he found out, how would the deception affect him? Could he afford to feel as though he couldn't even trust me? And if I didn't tell the children, how could I possibly pursue Dan without their knowing?

I tried to think through all of the implications of telling them and not telling them, but my own outrage at Dan made it hard to reach a rational decision. Finally I opted for the middle of the road; I called Dan and gave him an ultimatum: I wanted the money, in cash, *today,* or I was telling the kids and then going to court. A part of me actually thought that might work, but I was wrong. We ended up going to court, and after more than two years I finally prevailed.

DISCUSSION OF BARBARA'S CASE

Developing strategies for collecting child support from a deadbeat parent are among the greatest challenges of welfare reform. There are numerous mechanisms for collection in force in all jurisdictions (discussed in this chapter), but the enforcement system is tremendously overburdened and billions of dollars still go uncollected each year.

A woman like Barbara is often faced with the dilemma that it ends up costing as much to pursue the deadbeat as she ultimately winds up collecting. It's difficult for one income to support two families, and it's not hard to find reasons not to pay this week or this month. When does a woman begin her pursuit? After two months, six months, more? When she's in such arrears on her expenses that her own credit is shot? There are no easy answers.

At this time, more than two dozen state and local agencies are involved in efforts to collect child support payments from parents who fail to pay. As part of a federal pilot program begun in 1995, approximately thirty state and local programs are involved in implementing changes to their child support enforcement systems, including seeking the cooperation of welfare recipients in establishing paternity, assisting unemployed parents who owe support in finding jobs, and even privatizing child support collection.

One enforcement proposal being debated in Congress proposes revoking driver's licenses of parents in arrears on child support payments. At the state level, nineteen states currently use this method as well as the threat of revocation of professional licenses of doctors, lawyers, real estate brokers, and others. How effective these programs are is not yet clear, but what is more certain than ever is the communities' growing commitments to dealing with deadbeats.

DEVELOPMENT OF A NATIONAL SCANDAL

A generation ago when women naturally expected that they would assume custody of their minor children, they also expected that their former husbands would be obligated to support the family. Many single-parent families were able to live on the alimony and child support obtained from ex-husbands, at least while the children were dependent. Their standard of living markedly decreased in many cases, as the economic burden of divorce has always affected women and children disproportionately. But if a man wanted a divorce, alimony and child support were part of the package.

Today the realities are different. In the large majority of cases, women continue to be the primary caretakers of minor children. The difference is that today few families can live on the support provided by ex-husbands, even when court-ordered payments are made, which is all too often not the case. This problem reached crisis proportions by the early 1980s, when it was considered a "national scandal" that so few fathers were required to pay adequate support and so few children were receiving the support that was ordered. What had happened was that courts were awarding inadequate amounts of support and, even more disturbingly, they were failing to enforce the awards that were made. For example, the U.S. Department of Health and Human Services (HHS) estimates that 27 billion dollars of child support that was awarded was uncollected in 1992.

FEDERAL LAWS THAT ADDRESS CHILD SUPPORT

In response to great political pressure, Congress intervened in the area of child support, which is almost exclusively within the domain of individual states. In 1975 Congress approved Title IV-D of the Social Security Act. Title IV-D was responsible for the development of a federal enforcement agency known as the Office of Child Support Enforcement. It also charged each state with establishing local offices for child support enforcement. The services that became available under the Title IV-D program included:

• parent locator services (to locate parents who disappear without fulfilling child support obligations;
• paternity (or parentage) establishment (to help determine who the financially responsible parents are);
• modification of support mechanisms (to keep awards current with the needs of the children and the ability of the parents).

In response to escalating costs and a child support system seemingly out of control, Congress amended the IV-D program with the Child Support Enforcement Amendments of 1984 and the Family Support Act of 1988. The purpose, of course, was to improve the services available in each state. Congress ordered every state to set forth (for individual courts) specific statutory guidelines to determine child support and to beef up mechanisms for collecting it. The laws required that states set forth specific formulas in order to ensure a substantial amount of uniformity among awards to prevent different courts from imposing inconsistent obligations on similarly situated individuals.

The guidelines vary from state to state, but generally three different models are used. For example, in about fifteen states courts are to award a flat percentage of the noncustodial parent's (usually the father's) income. It can be calculated in terms of gross or net income, as long as the courts are consistent.

More than thirty states use an income share guideline. This is more complicated, because it takes into account the income of both parents as well as child care and other expenses. The support amount is figured by looking at both the income of the noncustodial parent and that income's relationship to the combined income of both parents. Determination of the award also takes into account the fact that as total family income increases, the percentage allocated to childrearing expenses usually decreases.

Finally, a few states use a formula that accommodates many more factors, including the obligations of the payor (such as financial responsibility for another family). In general, a court will determine the amount necessary to meet the basic needs of the children and then add a standard-of-living adjustment to the extent that additional income permits. Courts may be given more or less discretion to deviate from the guidelines, but once again the awards must be consistent.

AFDC

As part of the Social Security Act, the federal government has long provided funds to assist financially needy families with children through its Aid to Families with Dependent Children (AFDC) program. AFDC is, in essence, a federally funded child support program that provides support for families with (a) dependent children and (b) an absent parent. In 1984, Congress decided that it would try to reduce AFDC obligations by pursuing delinquent fathers and making them support their dependent children. With this incentive, Congress made sweeping changes to the federal laws, specifically the 1984 Child Support Enforcement Amendments and later the Family Support Act of 1988.

With the enactment of these federal programs, the federal government assumed an active role in the enforcement of child support. For example, under Title IV-D the Office of Child Support Enforcement (OCSE) was established. Significantly, however, the role of the federal government continued to be limited to overseeing states' administration of their own plans. The federal government assisted by coordinating cooperation among states, but a major problem with the present system has always been that once a deadbeat dad leaves the state, interstate enforcement of awards is difficult to enforce. As this book goes to press, legislation has been proposed specifically to deal with this problem. See page 83.

OBRA

The most recent efforts of the federal government to help the states deal with the child support crisis has been through the Omnibus Budget Reconciliation Act (OBRA), passed in 1993. The most relevant directive of OBRA is that states—if they wish to receive federal funding—must establish "expedited" procedures for determining paternity (or parenthood). (The states were already required to have expedited procedures for enforcing child support orders.) For example, the new regulations require that once the parent is located, the paternity procedure and the support order are to be in force within one year or less, regardless of whether the parent is in or out of state. One consequence of trying to expedite the process has been that states now use decision makers (sometimes known as "masters" or "referees") other than judges in order to comply with the federal requirements without overburdening the state court systems.

There are other important facets of OBRA that help determine a child's parents and establish a support order. In particular, OBRA requires hospitals to establish various outreach programs designed to encourage the fathers of children born to unmarried women to voluntarily acknowledge their fatherhood. One such program is to make genetic testing available (at the hospitals where children are born) to any man who does not know, but is willing to find out, whether in fact he is the father of the child and is willing to be tested. The test may be offered at little or no cost. Another is to establish a mechanism for men to "sign up," i.e., indicate that they recognize being a child's father. This requires that the father understand the rights and obligations of parenthood. If, after being so informed, a man freely claims a child as his, a support order might then be based upon that acknowledgment.

AFDC AND STATE MANDATES

The federal guidelines were designed in response to some startling statistics concerning the support of children in single-parent homes. For example, it is estimated that 87 percent of families receiving AFDC end up on the public dole because they do not get sufficient child support from the natural fathers. It is also estimated that less than 60 percent of children of divorce have been awarded any support at all and that less than half of those receive full payment and nearly a third of those receive nothing at all. It is also estimated that, after divorce, the standard of living of mothers and children declines by up to 70 percent, while the standard of living of fathers tends to increase up to 40 percent. There is no question that the breakup of a family is responsible for a great portion of the poverty in this country, and that failure to get or enforce child support awards is a major contributing factor.

Melissa had two children, ages three years and fourteen months, when her husband, Stanley, left the marriage. They worked out a financial arrangement, but the payments for child support are totally irregular. If Stan has an unexpected car repair, he doesn't pay support that month; if he decides to buy a gift for the children, he deducts it from child support. And many months he simply pays nothing at all, usually offering one excuse or another and sometimes none at all. Melissa tried to sign up for public assistance, but did not meet the eligibility requirements because she does get some support, even though it is sporadic. Melissa is unable to make it on her own but also unable to enforce the child support order because she cannot afford to pay a private attorney, even one of the least expensive ones. She tried to get publicly assisted legal aid, but it had been cut back so much that it also appeared virtually unavailable to her. At one point Melissa even tried to represent herself, but found that, procedurally, handling a child support case without a lawyer was much too complicated.

The enforcement programs that Congress developed and required states to adopt in some form (in order to keep getting AFDC for its residents) have a number of standard provisions. As discussed above, one is that each state must adopt some form of standardized child support guidelines to ensure that the awards are fair, adequate, and consistent; a second provision requires that states implement specific mechanisms to help track down delinquent parents when a support order is in effect and is not being honored. A third major requirement is that states provide collection services for families on AFDC. This not only helps get families off of public assistance, but it also reimburses AFDC for the money that it paid out in the event that delinquent parents are found and child support payments are collected.

Finally, current laws require that states also assist non-AFDC families who request help in enforcing and collecting child support payments. This is Congress' attempt to prevent welfare dependency in the first instance by helping dependent families to collect the child support that is due. Prior to 1984, the states were only required to help families collect delinquent support payments if they were on AFDC (so that AFDC would be reimbursed). The direction of this new law is toward requiring parental responsibility in all instances, leaving the welfare system as a course of last resort.

States on their own have set up other services to assist families in locating absent parents through records, employment, and other leads. States have also developed specific tactics for collecting and distributing child support payments in specific cases and for getting delinquent fathers into court, establishing appropriate awards, modifying child support awards where necessary, and, most important, getting payments made. Each state has developed and implemented its own specific measures to try to fulfill the various objectives. For example, some states now draw their information from such sources as the Department of Motor Vehicles, credit bureau reports, property listings, and even quarterly wage statements from the Internal Revenue Service. To support these activities, the federal Office of Child Support has established a Parent Locator Service, which is able to access data contained within a number of the federal agencies and to use that information to assist custodial parents in collecting child support.

In making the states conform to its requirements, Congress attempted to give each state a substantial amount of leeway in creating and implementing processes and procedures that would work best in each system. Congress did make some specific requirements, one of which was to establish a national, centralized system for tracking and monitoring child support payments to eliminate many of the disputes over such questions as how much is due, when it is due, whether it was paid, etc. Usually this is accomplished by setting up some sort of central clearinghouse that stores and retrieves this information. More important, however, a central location can assist with the specific programs for collecting delinquent payments, such as through wage assignments, wage reporting, tax refund intercepts, and similar mechanisms (discussed in a later section) that require centralized and computerized records.

SUPPORT WHILE LIVING APART

Many states have simplified their procedures for helping both married and unmarried persons living apart to obtain child support.

Jenn was separated from her husband, Peter, when their daughter was nineteen months old. Jenn had not worked since before the child was born, and she was completely dependent upon Peter for support. Hoping that Peter would eventually return to the marriage, Jenn didn't want to go to court and start divorce or even legal separation proceedings, but the money Peter gave her just wasn't enough to live on.

Jenn ultimately found that in her state she could get a support order just by following a procedure simple enough to be done without a lawyer. In her case, a clerk in the court assisted her and she managed to get a temporary order of support, which Peter ultimately obeyed.

To obtain an order for temporary support, for example, the petitioning party need only establish that (1) paternity is not contested, (2) the parties are living apart, and (3) one or more children are living with the parent seeking support. If everything is in order, many courts will issue a temporary order, and it does not even matter whether the other parent shows up in court.

HOW SUPPORT AWARDS CAN BE ENFORCED

Virtually the most difficult part of the child support process is in enforcing the order, a detail Congress recognized when it set about to overhaul the child support system. As part of the 1984 Act, Congress required that states implement certain specific measures and undertake to establish and fund the programs that required federal participation. Still other measures were suggested but without a clear mandate that the states adopt them:

1. *Income or wage assignments.* If there is a support order in effect and payments have been delinquent for a period of time, and if the court believes it is necessary to ensure timely payments, it can order a wage assignment. The support money is deducted by the employer from the employee's paycheck along with all other payroll deductions. Depending upon the court order, the money may be forwarded directly to the custodial parent. If for any reason this is unacceptable or unworkable, it can be sent by the employer to the court or to the state department of revenue, whatever the court decides.

    According to the 1984 Act, wage assignments can be applied to any type of "periodic income," specifically including disability benefits, pension benefits, annuities, workers' compensations, insurance proceeds, partnership profits or interest, dividends, or trust income. The important provision is that a stream of income be regular and periodic and that it be paid by someone who will be responsible and accountable for getting the money to the dependent children, the court, or the state department of revenue, whichever is ordered.

2. *Direct wage withholding.* One of the most effective methods of collecting child support related to wage assignments is through wage withholding. This is used in those cases in which child support payments are delinquent in an amount equal to one month of support. The law requires that the employer be notified and ordered to withhold the employee's wages in accordance with a "provisional wage withholding order." If the

employer should fail to do so, it can be held responsible for the amounts that were not withheld. In fact, in some states employers are fined for failing to withhold wages in accordance with a proper order. This type of order can be used in several types of proceedings—including divorce, paternity, and separation—and is useful because it can be instituted in the shortest possible time frame.

3. *W-4 reporting of new hires.* While all states now have mechanisms for wage withholding, if an absent parent moves out of state, it is estimated to take between thirteen and twenty weeks for a withholding order to take effect with a new employer. During this time support is often not paid, and some delinquent parents simply move on to a new job once the order does catch up with them. In order to expedite the process of establishing new employment, some states have implemented a mechanism whereby new hires would indicate on their W-4 forms whether or not they have an outstanding child support obligation, the amount of the order, and the payee, in which case the withholding begins immediately. If an employee fails to report his support obligation, he is subject to a criminal penalty. Approximately ten states currently use this provision, and several others are considering similar laws.

4. *Tax refund intercept.* In cases in which the person ordered to pay child support is an employee who has state and/or federal taxes withheld from his pay and a refund is generally due, it is possible to intercept either a state or federal refund. It is available to AFDC and non-AFDC parents. Although this process is not realistic against all delinquent parents (because of various procedural obstacles and eligibility requirements), it has proved to be valuable recourse for those custodial parents who are owed support and when delinquent parents meet the intercept requirements. For example, in 1985 more than 489,000 refunds were intercepted, amounting to approximately $240 million of delinquent child support payments.

5. *Attachment of property.* If a delinquent parents owns real property (i.e., a home or real estate) or has a valuable asset (e.g.,

a car), it may be possible to "attach" the property (which means to "hold" it to secure the debt) and ultimately to have it taken and sold to pay the debt. This requires a court proceeding but is relatively straightforward as long as valuable and marketable assets can be found.

6. *Liens on property.* Similar to an attachment, a lien can be placed on real or personal property, which prevents it from being sold until the lien is satisfied (and thereby discharged). These are useful in those cases in which wage assignment or withholding was not possible but the delinquent parent does have assets that can be found.

7. *Trustee process.* Like attachments, this requires that the custodial parent who is owed support be able to find property. In this case the property must be a bank account, stock brokerage account, or other liquid asset that is within the control of a third party (e.g., a bank). The actual procedure is similar to that of attachments and requires that a court order be secured after the account is located. As is also true of attachments, the process is more complicated if the asset is located out of state.

Additional remedies that might be available, particularly against self-employed and professional deadbeats, include revocation of professional or occupational licenses or mandatory credit bureau reporting. Attachments and liens on property may be possible when a delinquent parent is self-employed and it is difficult to reach income in other ways.

For the most part, these collection methods are similar or identical to those used to collect any debt. In fact, in recent years, a number of custodial parents who are owed substantial sums of money in uncollected support are turning to private collection agencies to try to obtain the money due. Although the same mechanisms are available through the appropriate state and federal agencies, some people find that private collection services are more effective in accomplishing the task. With an estimated $19 billion of child support going uncollected each year, there is ample motivation for those private companies actively to pursue delinquent parents.

INTERSTATE ENFORCEMENT OF CHILD SUPPORT

Among the most troublesome aspects of collecting child support today is trying to obtain and enforce a support order against a delinquent parent who has left the state. The law provides many uniform acts that are set forth as models to promote similar and consistent laws that affect people who are trying to engage in transactions across state lines. Although no state is obligated to adopt a uniform act, most states do so in some form (unless it is contrary to some important state policy). These acts generally contain provisions for cooperation and reciprocal enforcement so that if state A and state B pass similar statutes (as suggested by the uniform act), each is likely to provide the other with whatever assistance it may require to enforce its provisions when residents move from state A to state B or vice versa.

The federal government has, through various programs, attempted to coordinate interstate support. In 1950, the Uniform Reciprocal Enforcement of Support Act (URESA) was created in order to assist a custodial parent in enforcing a child support award across state lines. Its primary purpose is to secure support payments for dependent children whose legally obligated parents have left the state that ordered they pay support. URESA provides, in general, that once an order of support is set initially by one state (the "initiating" state) and the parent moves to another state (the "responding" state), the responding state will not change the order but will enforce it in the same amount previously set by the initiating state. The major purpose of URESA is to prevent "forum shopping."

David was ordered to pay $1,800 per month for the support of his three minor children, in addition to maintaining health insurance and assisting with uninsured medical expenses. He thought the amount ordered was exorbitant, particularly since his brother,

who was in a similar situation in another state, paid
nearly half as much in support. David thought that the
particular judge was unfavorable to him and that if he
were in another state, particularly his brother's, it
would treat him more favorably. He eventually moved,
hoping to get a new order or a modification of the old
one by a more liberal court.

Under URESA, states are forbidden from entering a support
order that supersedes or changes an order from a previous court.
The one issue that either parent can contest, however, is whether
the initiating court had the right to enter a judgment in the first
place (i.e., whether the court had jurisdiction). If ultimately the
determination is that the support order was rightfully created by the
initiating court, the order is thereafter entitled to "full faith and
credit," meaning that the responding state is bound to accept and
enforce it.

It is also important to realize that a lawsuit brought under
URESA only operates to enforce an existing child support order.
All remedies under the act are in addition to whatever other
remedies may be available under either state's laws. URESA,
therefore, does not create an order for support; it only provides
another potential avenue for enforcing a support decree that has
already been ordered.

While URESA has gone a long way in helping interstate
enforcement of existing support orders, there is at least one major
problem that URESA has not been able to address: there is little
coordinated networking for communication between states to keep
track of cases once they are referred to another state. Most
communication that does occur is between one local court and
another. As a result, there is not a systematic procedure for keeping
track of the large number of cases that come through. Recent
federal legislation has attempted to remedy this problem, propos-
ing that states establish interstate computerized databases and
clearinghouses to record such information as the name, address,
income, and support order of a delinquent parent. Ideally, each

state would have a Registry of Support Orders to store an abstract of all case information, even though it would not be responsible for collection. Each state would register all incoming and outgoing requests for enforcement of child support from one state to another and would use and register such mechanisms for collection as wage withholding and other similar measures. The current law also requires states to make their wage assignment systems available for interstate support orders.

As this book goes to press, the House and Senate have approved sweeping new changes to the child support enforcement mechanisms. For example, a Uniform Interstate Family Support Act (UIFSA) would replace URESA. Under UIFSA, if either parent lives in the state that makes an initial award, that state keeps jurisdiction even if the other parent leaves. Therefore a mother does not have to chase a deadbeat dad to wherever he's gone in order to get a support order. Further, a garnishment order from one state can be mailed directly to the father's employer in another state, and be enforced. UIFSA also contains clear rules as to which state has authority to issue a support order, so that fathers cannot complain that they have two inconsistent orders from two states— a perfect excuse not to honor either obligation.

Another aspect of the new proposed legislation concerns paternity testing. See chapter 4. A controversial provision would eliminate the right to a trial by jury in all paternity cases, and establish a presumption of paternity on the basis of DNA testing. The effect would be to make it easier and less expensive for a mother to establish the identity of her child's father.

Since the House and Senate versions of this bill are not identical, a final version must still be worked out in conference and signed by the President. The climate is ripe, however, for legislative reform, and significant new laws are expected.

ENFORCEMENT OF LAST RESORT: CONTEMPT AND CRIMINAL NON-SUPPORT

If civil collection methods are not effective in helping custodial parents of dependent children receive their child support, the custodial parent may be able to institute an action for civil or criminal contempt. Contempt is a separate proceeding (distinct from obtaining the original support action) and usually requires the services of an attorney. A defendant will be subpoenaed to go to court and will be given the opportunity to explain why the support is not being paid. Unless he has a good explanation, however (e.g., he has lost his job and has no income), he will be held in contempt. (Technically, he can be held in contempt even if he does have an adequate explanation, because if he is unable to pay, his remedy is to go back to court and seek a modification of the decree, *not* simply to stop paying.) In any event, even if the defendant is adjudged to be in contempt, he might be jailed or fined, but usually the collection remedies are only those that are already available to support recipients.

Criminal nonsupport is a remedy of last resort, primarily because it results in the defendant's having a criminal record and subjects him to criminal penalties. Under the Child Support Recovery Act of 1992, it is now a federal crime for a parent who lives in a state that is different from that of dependent children to willfully fail to pay child support. While it is estimated that currently at least 500,000 cases could be prosecuted based on these terms, without the judicial resources to do so, in many cases the result has simply been that the law has not improved the probability of collecting the delinquent payments. Yet under the right circumstances the criminal law has proven to be a very effective tool. If a parent has the ability to pay and simply refuses, the threat (or reality) of criminal prosecution may encourage payment where no other method has worked.

Criminal laws vary from state to state, but criminal nonsupport generally requires (1) abandoning a minor child (or spouse) without making reasonable provisions for his or her support and (2) willfully failing to comply with an order of support rendered by a proper court for reasons other than inability to pay. The criminal penalty if a defendant is found guilty of nonsupport also varies from state to state. In some states it is a misdemeanor (i.e., a minor criminal violation); in others it is a felony (i.e., a serious criminal offense). Penalties can include fines and imprisonment or both. Many states impose harsher penalties in cases of interstate nonsupport where it appears that a defendant has fled a state specifically or primarily in order to evade a support obligation. Defendants in cases of criminal nonsupport can be arrested and extradited as child support delinquents. This means that state authorities take responsibility for apprehending and sending a defendant back to the state that ordered the support obligation. This is significant because defendants in civil cases can ignore summonses if they are out of the state, and it is virtually impossible to serve them across state lines. Without a summons, a defendant cannot be legally compelled to appear in court.

This criminal procedure is typically used only as a last resort in those cases involving defendants with long histories of nonpayment who have the ability to pay and who have left the state and refuse to comply with a local order of support. Offenders can be listed in the National Crime Information Center (NCIC), which is a national register of individuals charged with a criminal offense.

CONCLUSION

As this book goes to press, Congress is still debating the question of how to better enforce orders of child support. One suggested remedy is to make it a federal offense to fail to pay support, thus avoiding the dilemma of state sovereignty and eliminating moving out of state as a way of moving away from the reach of the court order. Clearly Congress is renewing its commitment to parental responsibility for minor children. If for no other reason, it simply no longer has the funds to pay the enormous costs of the social programs that pick up the bill when parents abandon their obligations. Today Congress appears convinced that the best solution is to vigorously pursue absent parents and remove incentives that encourage deadbeat dads to abscond without paying child support obligations. The best strategy appears to be predictable enforcement with potent penalties for willful noncompliance.

Currently, the focus is on interstate enforcement since it is the area that has the least effective remedies.

6

Child Custody Alternatives and Their Impact on the Payment of Support

In the days of fault-based divorce, mothers expected that they would assume the custody of their minor children and fathers would provide support. The law had indoctrinated a "maternal preference" for child custody, particularly when the children were "of tender years." Unless the mother was proven to be unfit, it was virtually impossible for a father to contest his traditional role. This arrangement provided some measure of predictability for the children and minimized the likelihood of what is known as "custody blackmail"—bitter parents using child custody to win financial concessions in the divorce settlement. With the advent of no-fault divorce, however, divorcing couples no longer had to negotiate the grounds for their divorce, and the fate of the children was no longer certain.

The reasons for the traditional rules of child custody were many. Fewer women were employed outside the home, and there was a natural continuity of child care for a woman to retain custody. Men participated minimally in the day-to-day care of children, and they were generally considered to be less nurturing and less suited for child care. Few men contested the issue, since male role models didn't teach men that child care was an important part of the male tradition.

In recent years, domestic relations law has evolved considerably and a number of changes have occurred. First, the unofficial "maternal preference rule" and "tender years doctrine" were challenged. They were said to discriminate against men, and the courts agreed. At least in theory, courts must give both men and women a fair opportunity to make their bid for custody. Second, the assumption that most women stay at home and fathers earn most of the household income is no longer borne out by the evidence. Today women are regularly employed in the work force. Whether through necessity or because of a desire for a better standard of living, more than half of all mothers no longer assume the traditional role of homemaker. Third, the assumption that women are somehow more nurturing and better overall custodial parents, even of young children, has been challenged. Many men in the 1990s are more comfortable with the male image of devoting large blocks of time, even stalling careers, to participate more actively in the upbringing of their children. Some feel that traditional male roles have deprived them of showing their "mothering" qualities.

Finally, with the collapse of the traditional fault-based divorce schemes (discussed in chapter 3), which required men to negotiate for the right to obtain a divorce, more men have challenged the courts' universal habit of awarding sole custody to the mother. Many such challenges have been successful.

The result of these changed conditions is that increasing numbers of men are seeking to become the primary custodians of their minor children when the decision to divorce is made. Of course, not all men are motivated by the strong desire to parent or even by the best interests of their children. Nevertheless, more and more are actively pursuing custody and forcing courts to take a hard look at what is best for the children. Forced to abandon their automatic preference for maternal custody and faced with serious challenges by fathers, courts confront difficult custody choices with little guidance as to what is best for the separating family.

The evolution, however, has only come so far. Often with good reason, courts are skeptical when men seek sole custody of their children. They are sensitive as to whether their desire for custody is sincere or whether it is a ploy to gain financial concessions.

When Sarah's husband, Tom, filed for divorce, there was no discussion about the custody of their two children. Sarah worked part time and she had assumed most of the traditional child care responsibilities. After both had retained lawyers and settlement negotiations got underway, Sarah learned for the first time of Tom's intention to contest custody. Frightened by the possibility that he could prevail, however unlikely it was, Sarah jumped at the first financial offer of settlement that did not take custody away from her.

It is not uncommon for women, in particular, to "give in" to custody blackmail and forego a more suitable financial settlement for themselves (and their children) when faced with the possibility of losing custody. Of course, women, too, have been known to extract concessions by using custody as a bargaining chip when they want to give up custody. Furthermore, some men (and women) are simply more willing to gamble with custody when that is the cost of cutting their best deal. In most cases women can still count on being favored for child custody when they want it. As a result, even when both parents are fit for the task, men still have to expect to compromise.

Today the most common compromise is a cooperative parenting arrangement known as "joint custody." Joint custody was first introduced when equal rights for men and women started to become a serious issue in the courts. Legally, joint custody means that each parent gets substantially equal access, authority, control, and responsibility for the children and assumes that each parent will share in raising the children. It is not a quasi-legal "shared parenting" agreement, nor does it require an equal division of responsibility. It is merely an arrangement that gives both parents substantially equal legal rights and responsibilities as to the care, custody, and responsibility for the children.

Joint custody is often implemented under conditions that have many of the hallmarks of sole custody (e.g., the children live with the mother during the week and with the father on weekends). What is important is that parents are able to share in the amount of time spent with the children and retain shared control over the major decisions and obligations that affect their lives. For example, parents may both retain joint legal custody but have the children live with one parent, usually the mother. In some cases children may spend weekends and/or vacations with the father. In other cases the parents may alternate custody: children can spend blocks of days, weeks, or even months in one place and then transfer to the other place. The longer the time interval, however, usually the more disruptive it is for the children. In rare cases, children may actually spend half of the year in one place and half of the year in the other, especially if the parents are separated by a large distance and no other practical remedy is feasible. Many courts consider these arrangements highly disruptive for the children and even prefer no visitation to this type of arrangement.

Still another possibility, and one that is rarely approved by the court, is separation of the children, with each parent assuming virtual sole custody of one or more children, with visitation to the noncustodial parent. Many courts require compelling reasons for separating the children because it is another disastrous separation for them that can have severe psychological consequences.

Today more than thirty states have enacted some type of law that provides for joint child custody. Many courts seem to favor such an arrangement if it appears that the parties are willing to try to make it work. In particular, it requires that the divorcing couple be able to cooperate with each other in making decisions that affect the children and in implementing the mechanics of joint custody (e.g., transporting the children back and forth).

There are numerous benefits to joint custody in those cases achieving a workable arrangement. For the courts, it relieves them of the burden of making difficult custody choices, which they are usually not equipped to address. All too often custody battles become a battle of the experts, each claiming that one parent is likely to be the better custodian but with little evidence to back up the claim.

For parents, the long-range outcomes of joint custody have been somewhat better than sole custody arrangements, reducing the need for parents to return to court to enforce visitation and support awards. It also appears to affect the way that parents view their participation with the children after the divorce. In some cases it lessens the additional burden of care that falls on the custodial parent. In other cases it seems to diminish the likelihood that a non-custodial parent (usually the father) will not pay child support. In still other cases it seems to reduce the potentially damaging strain on the relationship between the noncustodial parent and children.

In many cases, however, it is difficult to know what is best for the children. Only hindsight can determine for certain whether divorced parents, when relieved of the burden of the deteriorating marriage, will interact with each other and the children in a way that allows the children to maintain a stable relationship with both. Joint custody is not indicated when there is continuing conflict and hostility between the parents that is exacerbated by the interaction necessary to implement this arrangement. Yet the court has only the short time of the hearing to observe and evaluate each of the parents and to speculate about what would be best for the children. For this reason, divorcing couples are urged to negotiate their own custody arrangements. Joint custody, in particular, is rarely an optimum solution if both parties will not agree to it themselves.

GUARDIAN *AD LITEM*

In cases of contested custody, courts in most states can appoint a guardian *ad litem* (temporary guardian) to represent the interests of the minor children. A guardian may be an attorney whose function is to seek out information concerning the needs and welfare of the children and to report the findings to the court. A potential guardian can be suggested by either parent or the judge and is ultimately appointed by the court to represent the children during the divorce proceeding.

Guardians perform a number of important functions. They talk to the children's parents, teachers, caretakers, relatives, guidance counselors, physicians, psychologists, or anyone else who may have knowledge about what is best for the children. They talk to the children. They must be willing to make an impartial inquiry and act on behalf of the children. Ultimately, their function is to report back to the court (i.e., testify) on behalf of the children.

One of parents' greatest fears about divorce trials is that the children may be asked to testify. A guardian can ensure that the children do not get in the middle if the custody battle gets bitter. In virtually all cases, children will not testify in open court. If they are old enough to express a preference, the judge may ask them to speak *in camera*, i.e., the judge will take their "testimony" privately, in his chambers, and what is said remains confidential. Very young children are rarely questioned at all, both to spare them the trauma of having to choose between their parents, and because their preferences are not given much weight anyway.

SOLE OR JOINT CUSTODY?

The relative merits of joint and sole child custody have been widely debated, and there is still much controversy about which is a better model and under what circumstances. Since the custody standard is always "the best interests of the children," courts are forced to evaluate the merits of the various options. Of course, not all parents seek custody and there are few cases that reach trial with child custody still contested. But when they do, courts are faced with difficult choices, often ones they must base upon subjective considerations. Assuming that both parents' desire for custody is sincere and not a tactic to coerce financial advantage, the court must consider, on a case-by-case basis, how joint or sole custody would operate for the particular family.

It has been argued that sole custody provides a permanent and unconditional placement of children, which is an essential factor in healthy child development. Advocates of this position urge courts to seek out and consider all factors, psychological as well as physical, that affect the question of which parent would best look out for the interests of the children. However, after making such a determination of who that sole custodian should be, some experts recommend the placement should be immediate, permanent, and unconditional. All decisions concerning the children should then be made by that parent. He or she should decide how, and under what conditions, the children should be raised, even including visitation by the noncustodial parent. The reason for this unilateral decision making is that despite good intentions, too many parents are just not able to cooperate with one another, and never-ending conflicts arise when decisions need to be made concerning the children.

Courts generally do not adopt such a radical position, particularly with respect to visitation. Recognizing the companionship rights of the absent parent, visitation is usually liberally granted to a noncustodial parent, primarily because it ensures an ongoing relationship with the child. As a practical matter, however, joint custody does sometimes create problems later on when inevitable changes occur. It is difficult for divorcing parents to predict what might happen in the future and what adjustments will need to be made. This is particularly difficult with joint custody.

Jill and David believed that they could make joint custody work for their three children. David was leaving the marital residence for Jill to live in with the children when they were with her. David was buying a townhouse in the same city that was adequate for his needs and could accommodate the children. The parties' anger and disappointment about the failed marriage, while evident, seemed under control. The children managed to move from home to home with minimal disruption until David remarried. After that, his townhouse was no longer big enough for all of them. The custody schedule was no longer stable as different things came up in David's household. Last-minute changes were frequent and disruptive. Jill, too, became less cooperative as new bitterness toward David was sparked by his remarriage.

It is not only residual hostility but also the practical problems of remarriage, change of residence, and return to the work force that disrupt mutual planning and decision making. Moreover, continued negative interactions between the former spouses often frustrate efforts to preserve the child's health and positive parent-child relationship that was at the heart of joint custody rationale. A serious danger for the children is the sense that they do not "belong" in either place or that neither parent is fully committed to their upbringing.

Betsy and Doug divorced when their daughter was three years old. Joint custody seemed ideal for them because their relationship was manageable and both adored the child and were willing to try to cooperate for her benefit. Joint custody worked well for the first two years until the child started school. At that point Betsy was obliged to go back to work to help make ends meet. She was not able to find work locally, however, and she ended up moving about fifty miles away. Betsy and Doug continued to try to work out joint custody but the commute made it difficult. Then there were the disputes over the location in which the child should attend school. Furthermore, as she grew older, she started to rebel against living in two different places where the lack of continuity made friendships difficult. After several years it was apparent that the child was paying too high a price for joint custody and again the family faced a difficult transition.

Wayne and Nancy were divorced when their twin boys were two years old. Joint custody seemed like a natural solution since both parents wanted a continued relationship with the children and Nancy was overwhelmed by the thought of sole custody of these two young boys. Shortly after the divorce, Wayne remarried and, although they continued joint custody, started taking on fewer and fewer days. Five months later, Nancy also remarried and became pregnant again. The greater obligations to the twins became burdensome and she was more insistent that Wayne uphold his share of the responsibility to them. In fact, neither parent assumed the role of sole custodian and the children were caught between two parents, both of whom had made new lives and neither of whom felt a primary obligation to their children.

There is another school of thought that views joint or shared custody and the needs of the children differently. Its advocates argue that joint custody, in appropriate cases, more intimately involves both parents in the raising of their children and prevents the child's sense of loss of the noncustodial parent. By alleviating some of the burden of care on the custodial parent, joint custody may result in a less stressful environment. Support payments are more regular, and typically not held hostage by a parent who is unable to visit with the children. Finally, joint custody may lead to a better sense of well-being because it may reduce the children's sense of being abandoned by the noncustodial parent.

HOW IS CUSTODY DETERMINED?

When child custody is contested, the parties are always encouraged to reach an agreement between themselves since it has been consistently shown that both the divorcing couple and their children adjust better to the divorce and are less likely to return to court with complaints of custody violation. Regardless of what the court decides, it is inevitable that at least one party (and sometimes both) will be unhappy with the court's decision and will be less willing to fulfill obligations to the children. In fact, bitter custody disputes outlive all other aspects of the divorce and no one ever really wins—certainly not the children.

At the same time one of the greatest fears of a woman facing divorce is the possibility that she could lose custody of her children. It is the unusual case, however, where a mother seeking custody will not at least be given joint custody. Only if she has a severe mental, emotional, or personality disturbance; a drug or alcohol dependency; a history of child abuse or neglect or a pattern of severe, erratic behavior toward the children would she be likely to lose sole custody to her husband. Nevertheless, the court is bound to award custody in the best interest of the children and to consider seriously a father's bid.

In those cases that custody just cannot be agreed upon, either because the parents are simply unwilling to compromise or because they cannot work out an agreeable solution, the court will be forced to decide for them. The question of what, exactly, the court looks for is not entirely clear. It is required to determine "the best interests of the children" but nobody really knows, in a particular case, what the deciding factors may be. There are certain circumstances, however, that are likely to be studied.

The court will inquire about who the primary caretaker is and what each parent does in terms of child rearing. Are the children physically cared for (food, clothing, schooling, age-appropriate activities)? If not, what is lacking and how would that be provided? The court will inquire about what ability and arrangements each parent would make to meet the physical and day-to-day needs of the children if custody were awarded to him or her.

The court will also inquire about the present relationship that each parent has with the children. It will need to know how each parent currently meets the needs of the children in terms of their existing parent-child relationship. Are the children well adjusted? Are they performing in school consistent with their capabilities? Do they interact well with friends and peers? The court will inquire about any problems that may relate to the child-rearing practices of either parent and the stability of the environment that has existed thus far.

The court will inquire about the physical and mental health of each of the parties. In particular, it will want to know if there is anything that is likely to cause a future disruption in the custodial arrangement once it is ordered. In this regard it is usual for both parties to provide a psychological expert—one who has examined that person and will report on his or her fitness to be a custodial parent. Since the linchpin of the custody determination is the "best interests" of the children, it is often critical testimony for each party that they be able to prove reasonable parenting skills. In cases where actual fitness is an issue, the court will appoint its own psychiatric expert to evaluate the parties.

The court will inquire about what major changes for the children would be required if sole or joint custody were awarded to either parent. How would present child care arrangements be disrupted? Is either parent planning to move away? Do the parents have the physical space for the children? And what type of plan would the custodial parent make for the children's visitation with the noncustodial parent? Courts often believe that they can determine whether the motives of parents vying for custody are sincere on the basis of their willingness to make the children available for visitation with their other parent.

If the children are old enough to express a preference, the court will usually allow them to do so in private. While there is no set cutoff for age, as mentioned earlier, very young children are usually not allowed to testify even if they choose to express an opinion.

Finally, the court will look at the overall home environment that each parent is likely to maintain. Are step-families currently involved and is either parent planning remarriage? What will that mean to the well-being of these children? What has the past environment been like? Has each parent maintained a stable presence or has past behavior been erratic? In many cases the answers to these questions will help determine whether each parent's desire for custody is sincere or whether the contest is being waged to gain some other concessions.

WHAT FACTORS ARE NOT CONSIDERED

In addition to all of the factors that the court will look at in making a custody determination, there are a number of issues that many parents, particularly mothers, become anxious about that usually will not affect the custody award. Among them are the fact that the primary caretaker up until that point will probably need to go back to work or has been working all along. The court will, of course, look at these factors, but generally it will not view in a negative light a woman's need or desire to be employed outside the house, as long as she makes reasonable provisions for the children. Interestingly, what a court will look at is whether she makes time for the special needs of her children while she also works. Does she take time off when the children are sick or have an appointment with the doctor? Does she participate in the children's recreational activities? Does she make their meals, shop for their clothing, and pay attention to their homework and schoolwork? The court usually will not be deterred from awarding custody to a woman who works as long as she actively cares for the children as well.

Another factor that courts generally will not consider is the fact that one parent, usually the father, can provide more material advantages for the children. The fact that the father will live in a bigger home, a better neighborhood, or simply has more disposable income to provide for the children is usually not important. In fact, if the court finds that one parent has been using his superior financial status (e.g., buying expensive gifts) to entice the children to express a preference, it is more likely to find that this is manipulation rather than an indication of superior or even sincere parenting.

Probably the most difficult issue to speculate about is the effect that a new relationship of either spouse will have on the custody determination. This will be discussed more fully in the next section ("When Custody Can Be Changed"), but it is not unusual for one or both parties, by the time of the trial, to have established a new relationship with someone else. What will be damaging is evidence of inappropriate or sexually explicit conduct in the presence of the children or evidence that the new liaison will disrupt that parent's ability or willingness to maintain a similar and stable child-parent relationship.

Courts do not look favorably on adulterous relationships before the spouses are divorced, but they primarily look at how the relationship affects the children. If it is causing them confusion or distress, then obviously that factor will be viewed negatively. Courts recognize, however, the inevitability of new relationships and marriages after the divorce and they do not necessarily cast aspersions on such a parent. In fact, if evidence of adultery or even a boyfriend or girlfriend has already been presented, a parent seeking custody may try to demonstrate the stabilizing effect that it would have on the children.

WHEN CUSTODY CAN BE CHANGED

Even after a child custody arrangement is agreed upon by the parties or ordered by the court, the court retains control (jurisdiction) over the case unless the children are lawfully removed from their residence to another state. The parties cannot agree to divest the court of its continuing control and either party can return to court at any time if the custody or support order is being violated or if a change in the order is warranted. As a result, even parents who are awarded custody often live under a continuing threat that the children might be taken away from them. But only rarely does it happen.

Changes in custody (or support orders, for that matter) can only be sought when a clear change of circumstances can be proved. In most states this requires that a new proceeding be initiated (e.g., Complaint for Modification), and it is usually costly since lawyers must once again get involved and start afresh. Court actions for modification are different from return visits to court to enforce an existing order. If a sole custodian refuses, for example, to adhere to the visitation schedule, the remedy is to go to court to enforce the order, not to modify it. If, however, there are repeated offenses by one parent, a modification of the original decree may be indicated.

The most common reason to seek modification today is that joint custody is not working or visitation is repeatedly denied. Often when visitation is denied, the noncustodial parent holds back support (which, incidentally, is illegal). If a custodial parent is denying the other access to the children, the remedy is to return to court to enforce the order or modify the decree, not to deny the child the support that is due. The court will then evaluate the circumstances and will issue a strong warning or hold that party in contempt of court, depending on the nature and frequency of the offense.

What will the court do if it appears that joint custody is not working? With an action for modification the court is required to review the circumstances anew, particularly in light of why the arrangement is not working. If either parent is clearly at fault, that parent is at greater risk for losing custody at that point. What happens more often is that the circumstances of joint custody, which appeared workable at the time of the order, are no longer satisfactory. Often when children get older, they object more to moving back and forth or living in two different places. At other times one or both parents has had to move. And sometimes the arrangement was simply ill advised and did not work from the start. If the court is satisfied that its original custody order is not in the best interests of the children, the parties will once again be encouraged to reach their own agreement or the court will impose its judgment on them. There are no easy answers, and they become tougher the second time around.

Another frequently litigated change of circumstance is the presence of a live-in companion of the custodial parent. As mentioned earlier, courts approach this matter in very different ways, but the critical issue should always be the effect that the relationship has on the children. In a highly publicized Rhode Island case, a court ordered a custodial parent to refrain from allowing any unrelated males from making overnight visits while the children were in the house. And yet in another state a court ruled that a mother could not be prevented from permitting overnight visits by unrelated males unless there was evidence that it directly affected the welfare of the children. Indeed, there is no single guiding principle for this issue except that courts are supposed to be looking out for the interests of the children rather than using these cases to impose their own morality. But what is "best" for the children is often a subjective consideration, and custody has been lost on the basis of a court's decision that the children would be better off in the other parent's household.

7

Deadbeat Dads and Single Moms: Who They Are

CASE STUDY: ERNEST

Having struggled to build a career for so many years, by the time I reached my mid-forties things were starting to pay off. In fact, life had been pretty good to me lately. My career finally seemed to be going someplace. For years, I had to struggle to get a dental practice started. I had to stick with it, working on weekends, networking, and charging low fees. But I was willing to do whatever it took to establish myself. I put everything second to the practice, including Karen, my long-time live-in girlfriend. Fortunately, Karen had a career of her own and was not particularly anxious to get married or have children. We gave each other a lot of space to develop our careers and only recently, with my business becoming stable, have I had some time to think about other things. In fact, Karen and I have begun to talk about getting married. We are both in our early forties and time is running out for having a child. But on the other hand neither of us is particularly child oriented; being a modern couple we are very involved with our own lives, and have resolved to develop our careers and have the good things in life that success brings. In fact, we had just come back from a ski vacation when I found the notification from the post office that I had a registered letter. I signed for the letter without any idea about what it contained, but when I read it I could see in an instant what a major impact it would have on my life.

Thirteen years ago I was in my last year of dental school and I was doing a clinical practicum at the dental school clinic. I was tired and anxious to finish up and get out into the world to earn some money. There was an attractive dental assistant named Janice who worked in the clinic, and almost as a distraction I started to flirt with her. As it turned out, she was just ending a difficult relationship and was interested in a man, particularly a professional man, who would pay some attention to her. Neither of us was interested in anything serious and we both seemed to enjoy it. It culminated with a brief affair which lasted all of maybe a week.

It was close to graduation when I recall getting a phone call from Janice. She said that she had missed her last period but that she would take care of things. I remember being mildly annoyed that I was being bothered at such a busy time when all I could think about was graduation and starting up a practice, and I'm sure I communicated that feeling to Janice. In any event, I never heard from her again, which was fine with me because I was looking forward to the freedom of no longer being a student and putting up with things that didn't interest me. I managed to put Janice's call out of my mind, and simply went on with my life. From time to time I did think about Janice and even wondered what she had done, but it seemed to be just a strange curiosity and I never dwelled on it. But when I read her letter I knew I had made a mistake.

Janice wrote that thirteen years ago when indeed she had become pregnant as a consequence of our brief affair, she could not bring herself to have an abortion. Being a woman of the '80s she felt that she could raise the child. She knew I was interested in getting on with my career and that I did not have any real interest in her so she decided to have the baby and raise it on her own. For better or worse, she seemed to have the help of a supportive family. To my amazement, she never intended to even let me know about our daughter. But in recent months the child had become persistent in asking about her father and was becoming increasingly emotional and distracted by her need to know about me. In the letter she said that she regretted never telling me about the child and seemed to recognize that she had been wrong to keep such a secret. Surprisingly, she didn't seem to blame me at all for being so negative when she tried to tell me that she might be pregnant. She did ask me to consider sending the child a picture of myself so that she could know what I look like and any other information that I might want to share. She said that the child wondered about whether I ever thought about her and, if so, what those thoughts might be. There was no mention about money nor any suggestion that I might want to have a relationship with the child. I sat there staring at the letter for several minutes, feeling both puzzled and bewildered. Could Janice be lying? Could she be telling the truth? A part of me was angry that Janice had contacted me, and a part of me was really scared. Mostly I was just numb because, although I didn't know what this would mean, I knew it would cost me a bundle. Just as I was beginning to realize some success, I was going to get taken to the proverbial cleaners.

After getting over the initial shock, I contacted my lawyer who put me in touch with one who specializes in paternity and child support cases in Janice's state. He did some preliminary investigation and then told me to brace myself for his findings. First, the state where Janice and the child live supposedly has the toughest child support laws in the country. In particular, he said that a child who has reached age thirteen can refuse visitation demands, meaning that she may never see the father who pays for her support. Second, his private investigator discovered that Janice did not hold any credit cards and did not own a car. If she did not pay any income taxes, it would indicate that she was probably on AFDC. He said that in that case, the federal government could come after me to reimburse what had been paid to Janice over the years. Finally, he recommended that I write to Janice right now and flatly deny being the father of her child.

This is where things stand right now. I feel angry and very

frightened about what might happen. I find that I have a slight curiosity about the child, since it's unlikely that I would ever have another one. But I also refuse to accept the responsibility for a child whom I was never allowed to know. Even though there is little question in my mind that the child is probably the product of our brief encounter, I have no intention of admitting that she is mine. I don't know what Janice's game is; maybe she's on the level, but I'm not going to take that kind of chance. If she wants something, she's going to have to come after me. I didn't want a child; I was not consulted about going ahead with the pregnancy and I certainly wasn't given any opportunity to be a father to the child. As far as I'm concerned, the child was Janice's decision. Why should I have my life ruined because of something that I did not know about and had nothing to say about?

If Janice got pregnant during our very brief affair, she must have lied to me about birth control. Certainly she hasn't had any problem deceiving me for all of these years; why should I believe that this wasn't her intention all along?

DISCUSSION OF ERNEST'S CASE

This case might just as well have been called the case of "Ernest and Janice" as it points to how in many cases the mother of the child participates with the father to create child support problems. Men often feel that it is the woman's job to use birth control or to make the "right" decision should an unplanned and unwanted pregnancy occur. If the woman chooses to give birth, the child is then hers and the man can feel justified in feeling no sense of responsibility to care or provide for the child. The actual existence of a child—a living, breathing, growing, feeling, thinking human being—is overshadowed by the father's anger, fear, and self-centeredness. Ernest is one type of man who feels trapped in the child support dilemma.

Janice, on the other hand, represents one type of woman who inadvertently colludes with the father of her child in such a way as to promote child support issues. In this case, Janice on her own chose both to have the baby and not to inform Ernest that he had fathered the child until many years later. In so doing she gave him every opportunity and ready-made excuses to deny and resist accepting responsibility. While men are often the culprits in child support and child support compliance problems, women who are passive, naive, or overbearing also can contribute to the problem.

The case of Ernest will in all probability turn out well for everyone. In contacting Ernest, Janice was very careful not to create an atmosphere of conflict. Her contacts with Ernest, both by letter and phone, have been low-keyed, non-demanding, and totally focused on the interests of her daughter. Realizing what a shock this would be to Ernest, Janice's approach was to give him ample time to get used to the idea of having fathered a child; to recognize his need to deal with his feelings of confusion, anger, and fear; and gradually to make the child real to him by sending Ernest information and pictures about the child, and then having him speak to the child directly. As this book goes to press, Ernest is in the process of doing DNA testing to definitively establish paternity and, depending on the results, is preparing to meet the child and her mother.

THE DEADBEAT DAD

Almost on a daily basis we read the newspaper headlines about fathers who have failed to pay their court ordered child support payments.

A father who failed to pay child support for his daughter, and then tried to claim part of an insurance settlement when she died, will go free as part of a court deal.

Nearly five decades after abandoning his wife and three young children, John G. has agreed to give her a small portion of the $5.1 million lottery jackpot he won in March.

A Michigan surgeon who owes more than $100,000 in child support for his 10-year-old daughter in Massachusetts became the target yesterday of a new federal law making it a crime to disregard support orders, federal authorities said.

A Colorado court has frozen a hefty installment of a lottery prize originally won by Albert T., one of Massachusetts' best-known deadbeat dads, to decide whether the money will go to Albert T.'s two teenage sons.

Providence—A man has been sent to state prison for falling more than $80,000 behind in child support payments to his ex-wife.

Officials said 1,314 absent parents who are delinquent on child support in Massachusetts earn more than $50,000 a year. Tax data show that 15,700 families would get off welfare if absent parents paid child support.

Uncollected child support payments are reported to be running at about $30 billion a year, directly affecting the lives of approximately 23 million children across the nation. Studies indicate that complete and regular child support payments are actually received in less than 50 percent of the cases in which there is court-ordered child support. The deadbeat dads have been so designated because roughly 97 percent of parents who are delinquent in making support payment are, in fact, men. They have also been called rats, weasels, scofflaws, and bums, and are viewed by some as shameful, unmanly and pathetic. But who are these men? Why do so many fathers become deadbeats and refuse to fulfill their obligations to their children? What kind of a man would refuse to provide support for a child that he has fathered? There appear to be identifiable factors that account for a father abandoning his financial responsibility to his child. There also appear to be patterns among delinquent fathers. It is only when these variables are understood that we can begin to look at things that can be done to facilitate the payment of child support.

WHO ARE THEY, AND WHY DON'T THEY PAY?

Until recently, little attention and few resources have been devoted to studying the issues associated with noncompliance with child support obligations (few men who have been criticized and scorned by society as much as these men are willing to come forward and volunteer themselves as research subjects). Consequently, much of what we know about them comes from the work of family counselors who, in their roles as therapists and healers, have taken the opportunity to make objective and non-judgmental observations. From this work a typology has emerged that describes four basic categories into which these men usually fall.

One category outlines what has been termed the "overextended parent." There are a number of variations of this type of man. The first is a man who was so eager to get out of his marriage or felt so guilty about leaving the marriage that he agreed to undertake an unreasonable level of child support that he was then unable to fulfill. This type of man is often described as relatively immature and naive, with little idea about what it takes to support two households. Once he falls behind on his support payments, it becomes virtually impossible for him to catch up. Thus the delinquency stems from his inability to meet the obligation, and often he eventually gives up even trying.

Bill never dreamed that sex could be so good until he met Rachel. He was inexperienced and she made him feel things he never felt before. It did not seem hard for him to leave his marriage and his children and he believed that he could take care of everyone. He soon found that keeping house with Rachel left little money for his ex-wife and children. He couldn't support both households.

The second variation largely includes men who start out paying the prescribed amount, but within a couple of years—often after comparing notes with other divorced fathers—they come to believe that their burden exceeds that which others are obliged to pay. This type of man is likely to become angry, but rather than go back to court to seek a modification of his payments, he unilaterally reduces the payment on his own. This type of man does not perceive himself as a delinquent because some payment is still made, but it is inadequate to meet the needs of the children.

> Jake was diligent in making his child support payments until he joined a bowling league and began to talk to the other men. He found that some were not paying any child support and that the others were paying much less than he was. He felt that once again, his ex-wife was abusing him, and the more he talked to the other men the angrier he became. One day he just made up his mind to cut his payments in half. He had convinced himself that she was lucky to get anything at all.

A third type of man who becomes an overextended parent is the noncustodial father who remarries, giving rise to a second family. When he has insufficient financial resources to meet the demands of both families, it is invariably his current family that gets taken care of and his noncustodial children that suffer.

> Tony was good about making his child support payments and was proud that he was continuing to take care of his children. When he remarried he was able to continue. It was more of a stretch for him financially, but he felt that as long as he had the money it was OK. Unfortunately, business took a turn for the worse about the time his new wife was giving birth. He felt he had little choice but to stop his child support payments and to take care of his new family.

As an aside, it has been observed that many men who have sufficient resources are often more diligent about making support payments when they remarry and have a second family. While this may be counter-intuitive, the reason may be that men who remarry are family oriented and consequently more concerned about the welfare of their children.

Finally, the fourth variation of the overextended father is one who becomes ill or unemployed; instead of going to court and having his payments reduced or temporarily suspended, he ignores the situation, engages in denial to avoid dealing with his payment problem, and merely drifts into delinquency without assuming any responsibility for his plight. When the problem inevitably catches up with him, he is the one who feels victimized by the system and adopts a hostile, rather than conciliatory, posture.

> Cal made a decent living as a carpenter and regularly met his child support commitment until he had a fall and injured his back. The people he was doing work for were uninsured and the injury left Cal without an income. As his finances became tighter he gradually stopped the child support payments. His ex-wife was aggressive about getting the state to go after him and he began to feel harassed by a system that didn't care to understand his situation.

The second category of men who fail to comply with their child support obligations are those who seek revenge against their ex-wives. This type of man carries with him many grudges, grievances and unresolved feelings concerning his marriage and family situation. Withholding child support payments is one of his few means of expressing anger. By controlling the money he exercises power and control over his ex-spouse, continuing the hostilities that resulted in the divorce but that apparently were not resolved by it.

> Fred always felt put down by Stella when they were married. He felt that she took every opportunity to make him feel small and inadequate. She even once

had an affair on him and threw it up to him every chance she got. When they divorced Fred's anger didn't go away, and now he could get back at her with the child support payments. He knew she needed the money and it made him feel powerful to play games with the payments.

Since disagreement over money is a major source of conflict in many marriages, particularly those that fail, withholding money is a way of keeping those past disputes alive. Where there was a high level of conflict between the parents prior to their separation, there is likely to be a high level of unresolved conflict subsequent to the divorce. In such high-conflict cases, withholding child support payments is not an unusual way for feelings of revenge to be expressed. Also, men who feel that they have been unfairly treated by the court may believe that the financial settlement is unjust and that withholding child support payments is warranted.

Everybody involved in Louis's divorce, except Louis himself, was a woman. The lawyer, the clerks, and even the judge were females. He was sure that he got taken advantage of by them and he was determined to fight back by not making his payments.

These men feel discriminated against by the legal system, hostile toward the world, and believe their ex-spouses are responsible for the injustice. Little regard is given to the effect that this vengeful behavior has on the children.

The third category of deadbeat dads are those men who do not make child support payments because of the emotional pain that is wrapped up in the divorce process. There appear to be two types of situations that provide these men with a rationale for withholding child support. The first is the man's intense emotional reaction to his marriage falling apart and his becoming an absentee parent. His feeling shut out of the family is intensely painful to him, and one way of coping with his emotional distress is by distancing himself from the children.

> Frank never believed that his wife would actually go through with the divorce. He couldn't imagine not being with his children, and when she actually did it he was devastated. He couldn't seem to recover even with therapy, so he decided to try to get a fresh start by moving to a new environment. Not living so close to the family seemed to help him deal with his feelings, and the less he saw the children the less he thought about them.

The very process of establishing distance, which may be both physical and emotional, protects him from pain but also causes him to become alienated from the family. What then emerges is the rationale that since he is no longer part of the family, he need not assume any of the financial responsibility for it. Thus, to cope with the pain of losing custody of his children, he pushes them away and ignores their needs.

The second type of situation within this category occurs when there is a dispute over visitation. Here an otherwise caring father is denied the amount of visitation that he wants with his children and withholds support as a way of forcing his ex-spouse to acquiesce to his visitation requests.

> Pat and Liz never agreed on much when they were married and this didn't change when they were divorced. The court awarded Liz sole physical custody of the children and Pat constantly fought with her about seeing more of them. Liz didn't think much of Pat as a father and didn't want the children spending more time with him than was necessary. The only way Pat could try to get his way was to send the child support payments only after visitation. If Liz didn't let him see the children when he wanted to, he would not send the check.

Interestingly, most problems involving denial of visitation stem from conflicts around money and payments of child support. Visitation thus becomes the ball on the economic playing field. Despite the fact that in most cases child support is specifically not conditioned upon a right of visitation, the emotional pain experienced by the noncustodial parent often causes him to seek revenge by hurting the very children with whom he wants to visit. Often this leads to a cycle of nonpayment and denied visitation that is so detrimental to the best interests of the very children who are the subjects of the support and visitation.

The fourth and largest category of deadbeat dads are those fathers who simply behave in an irresponsible manner with respect to their children. This type of man may disappear, not because he is overburdened per se and not because he is angry or vengeful toward the mother of his children. Many simply have no interest in parenting. Their role models have either been extremely poor or nonexistent and, not having themselves been treated well as children, they feel no responsibility to care for their own children. They rarely think about the children and may not even think of themselves as the parent.

> Stan never wanted children and agreed to have them only to please his wife so that she would be more available to him sexually. He always considered them "her" children, and when his marriage ended he felt unburdened.

For this type of man, children have little meaning in his life and he feels little obligation on their behalf. He certainly would not go out of his way or change his established pattern of behavior, nor would he consider working harder to make more money in order to provide for the children. This category includes the father who participated in bringing a child into the world but who has little or no sense of what it takes to rear that child. This kind of man often feels as though he was trapped by the woman and therefore believes that he is entitled to abdicate responsibility for the child.

Finally, there is a small category of men who are said to be going through what has been termed the "New Life Syndrome." This type of man is egocentric and self-absorbed. While many deadbeat dads also tend to be self-centered, most seem to have some rationale for their behavior other than merely their own self-interest. This type of deadbeat is different: he needs no justification for his delinquency other than his own desires. He puts himself first; he feels entitled to have his needs met above all others, including his children; and he offers no excuses for his behavior.

> Terry always knew he had gotten married and had children at too young an age. He felt that he never had a chance to sow his wild oats. The divorce freed him from all of that and he eagerly explored the options his new life offered. To do all the things he had dreamed about doing required money and he was determined to move ahead even if others went without. He had sacrificed so much for his ex-wife and children and he felt that now it was his turn to live and that was that.

OTHER FACTORS RELATED TO COMPLIANCE

The personality and emotional maturity of the noncustodial father, as outlined above, is clearly a major contributing factor in the nonpayment of child support. It is not, however, the only factor. Divorce usually is difficult for even the most mature, stable, and responsible men. They must often deal with the acute emotional crisis created by the divorce, redefine their self-image of husband and father, and develop a new social support system of their own. When divorced fathers are asked directly about their compliance with their child support payments, some significantly overstate their degree of compliance, but many report taking their responsibility seriously. When asked about what they believe to be sufficient reason to withhold payments, most men only acknowledge two such reasons: when a man is unemployed, and when his ex-wife uses the money for herself and not the children. Among men who report making full payments most of the time, most said that they did not see any other legitimate reason for not paying child support. For example, they did not feel that anger at an ex-spouse, having a new family of their own, being overextended, or not being able to participate adequately in child-rearing practices were sufficient grounds for withholding child support. Such men portray themselves as being reliable and responsible fathers, leading to the assumption that other rationalizations for not paying child support appear to be largely associated with a father's immaturity and emotional instability. This, however, may not be the case. A number of scientific studies have concluded that compliance dwindles over time and that numerous other factors play a significant role in this happening. Thus, what fathers say is not necessarily an accurate measure of what they actually do.

An important variable in maintaining child support obligations is the father's employment status. If a father is unemployed it is likely to be more difficult for him to make his child support payments. But even when a man is employed, income per se is not a significant or determining factor for compliance. Many men with incomes of $50,000 a year or more fail to make regular payments, and many make none at all. High income alone does not guarantee compliance; a sense of commitment and responsibility toward the children is much more important. A man who has a strong sense of concern and obligation for the well-being of his children is much more likely to share his available financial resources.

Yet another significant factor is the father's perception of how much control he has in determining how his child support payments are used on behalf of the children. For example, if he believes that his child support payments are being used by his ex-spouse on herself, he is less likely to continue making payments. Some men who feel that they have little say in the children's upbringing believe it is ample excuse for not meeting financial responsibilities.

When there is joint child custody, a factor often related to compliance with child support obligations is the length of time that the children live with the father. When children stay with the father for periods of weeks or even months at a time (such as on holidays or school vacations), there is a tendency for payments to be withheld or reduced at those times because the father perceives himself as already supporting the children.

Extended visits are frequently viewed by fathers quite differently than shorter stays, because of the length of time and cost involved. Yet this may be inevitable when father and children live geographically distant from one another. The children have to travel far to visit their father, and therefore the visits tend to be less frequent but longer.

Often this changes, however, as children get older. Adolescents become reluctant to leave their friends for extended periods, resulting in their visits with fathers becoming less frequent. The reduced time together is likely to diminish the emotional connection between father and children, and the resulting alienation serves to diminish the father's commitment to meeting his child support obligations. While this is not universally true, the level of contact between a father and his children is generally considered to be a significant factor in child support payments being made. Men who see their children irregularly are more likely to abdicate their financial responsibilities to them.

The remarriage of either or both spouses often creates another obstacle to continued child support payments. If the mother remarries and the ex-husband continues to maintain hostility against her, he may feel betrayed and angry at her new relationship. Her remarriage gives him an excuse to terminate payments upon the rationale that her new husband will provide for the children and his support is no longer necessary. This is a typical reaction when it is the *ex-wife* who remarries. When it is the ex-husband who remarries, there seem to be two possible paths. When economic resources are limited, a father is often faced with the difficult task of trying to maintain a good standard of living for his new family while at the same time struggling to keep up with his child support payments, which his new wife will often pressure him to reduce, or even stop. On the other hand, fathers who have an adequate income when they remarry frequently continue to make their child support payments, particularly if they are able to maintain a relationship with the children.

A very important consideration that affects full and timely child support obligations being met is the prior and existing relationship between the children's mother and father. Factors include: the length of the marriage, the quality of the relationship during the divorce process, and the continuing level of attachment and interaction between the parents. Marriages that lasted a long time appear to result in a greater financial and emotional investment on the part of both parents. This interdependency between the parents may foster or facilitate an enduring attachment between them, which thereby reinforces their commitment to cooperate in the upbringing of their children. By the same token, parents who relate to each other in a relatively non-hostile manner during the divorce process also increase the likelihood that support will be paid. A poor quality of relationship between the ex-spouses often gives rise to the father expressing his negative feelings through noncompliance with support obligations. Thus, to the extent that a good relationship between former spouses can be maintained, it will reinforce the mutual commitment to their children and is likely to lead to greater compliance with child support obligations.

Another element that is likely to influence the continuity of child support is whether the obligation was arrived at by agreement or by court order. An agreement generally gives both parties an opportunity to exercise some control over the amount and frequency of the payments. This reduces the likelihood that the father will feel that he has been treated unjustly by the legal system. A feeling of being victimized often provides an excuse for not fulfilling financial responsibilities to the children.

Perhaps the single most important component is the degree of likelihood that the order will be enforced. Many fathers will not voluntarily pay child support to their ex-wives unless they are confronted by an authority that is willing and able to track them down and employ enforcement mechanisms. Compliance rates are significantly higher when there is a court-monitored system for collecting child support and where there is a certainty of recourse (e.g., fines and/or jail) for noncompliance. In the absence of a perceived direct relationship between nonpayment of child support and punishment, many fathers simply will not pay. The burden of collecting child support still falls primarily upon the mother, whose responsibility for pursuing payments that are in default often seems overwhelming and unmanageable. Many women become discouraged with having to deal with a slow and generally unresponsive legal system, trying to locate the whereabouts of an ex-husband, and finding the time, energy, emotional strength, and financial resources to carry a legal action forward.

It is currently estimated that deadbeat parents, primarily fathers, owe 30 billion dollars nationally in unpaid child support. Despite what divorced fathers say about their commitment to support their children, estimates of non-compliance with child support payments are that it ranges from 50 to 80 percent. This invariably results in a decline of the standard of living for the children, with profound and enduring consequences to their social, educational, and emotional development. Nonsupport seriously compromises the ability of a child to get a decent start in life. A study published by the National Child Support Assurance Consortium reported that during the first year after a parental breakup (the time period when many fathers *will* comply with child support payments), 55 percent of children missed regular health checks, 36 percent were unable to obtain medical care when they became ill, 37 percent lacked appropriate clothing, 26 percent were left unsupervised while mothers went to work, 49 percent could not participate in school activities due to lack of money, and 32 percent went hungry at times. While, undeniably, there are real circumstances that may lead to a father's inability to support his children (even with families that are intact), most non-supporting fathers *can* provide for their children but fail to do so because of the reasons previously discussed: self-centeredness, emotional immaturity or instability, disconnectedness from the lives of their children, unresolved conflicts and mistrust of their ex-wives, and the lack of legal recourse against them.

THE SINGLE MOTHER WHO DOESN'T RECEIVE SUPPORT

In most states the burden of collecting child support still falls upon the parent, and how she responds to a deadbeat dad has a significant impact on the likelihood of her obtaining child support payments. Indeed, the attitudes and responses of many custodial mothers contribute to the problem. Those who do not pursue child support in an effective and timely fashion reinforce, to both themselves and the deadbeat dad, that they are either unwilling or unable to stand up for the rights of their children. There are several types of women whose reactions or inaction contributes to the problems they encounter in receiving child support payments.

One type of woman is inappropriately passive and believes that someone will come along and take care of her. These women are often young and may never have had the responsibility of living on their own. When their relationship or marriage ends, they naively believe that the children's father will continue to provide financial support. It is a rude awakening indeed when he does not, and often for the first time she finds herself on her own. She must assume sole support of her children or figure out a way to get the father to pay his share.

> Debbie and John were very much in love. Even though they were only sixteen years old, when Debbie became pregnant they decided to have their "love child." Debbie never questioned the fact that John would take care of her and the baby until she had given birth and it was too late to do anything else. John couldn't get a job to pay enough to provide for Debbie and the baby, and even though he always told her he would do better, he never did. She became preoccupied with taking care of the baby and John drifted away, out of their lives. He sort of dissolved and Debbie was at a loss as to what to

do next.

Many such women attempt to engage a lawyer, but soon realize such a route is complicated and expensive. Others find the responsibility for pursuing a legal remedy when payments are in default to be overwhelming and unmanageable. They find that they must deal with a slow and generally unresponsive legal system. But for so many women, finding the time, energy, emotional strength and financial resources to carry the legal action forward is more than they can muster.

Passive women also fail to follow through with the federally funded agencies that are available to provide assistance. While the services provided by these agencies are generally free of charge, they require monitoring and persistence, since the case workers are generally overburdened and the process is typical of large bureaucracies. A woman who relies on federal or state services must be prepared to pursue the case workers on a regular basis and insist that all available avenues of recourse be exhausted.

A second type of woman who may encounter difficulty in working through a bureaucratic government agency is the woman who is anxious and angry. She frequently deals with her frustrations poorly by flooding the child support agency with highly emotional calls and letters and by irritating the case workers who are overwhelmed with cases but who are nonetheless trying to help.

Frances had been neglected throughout most of her life, and her inability to get the state to act on her behalf and find her ex-husband and force him to make his child support payments was just another example of this. But this time she was not going to sit helplessly by and do nothing. When her case worker told her that he was doing everything he could and that he had dozens of cases like hers to handle, she would not let him dismiss her so easily. At first she just acted with persistence, called him frequently for progress reports and visited his office regularly to let him know she was not going to go away. She contacted the supervisor, but to no result. Finally her frustration got the better of her and one day she started screaming hysterically at her case worker. She was still unable to get results and her emotions got the better of her. She relentlessly and emotionally pursued her case worker and his supervisor. When they saw her coming they would leave the office and tried to avoid having any contact with her even though they would have liked to help her.

While the long-held maxim that "the squeaky wheel gets the grease" may be true in many instances, this type of woman tends to be so overemotional and overbearing in her efforts to gain assistance that she actually works against herself as she alienates the very people who can help her.

Ava thought that when the court ordered her ex-husband to pay child support that she could relax and devote herself to her children. Then when he left the state and it took months to locate him, she believed now he would have to do what was ordered. But she became very disillusioned when, after all his avoidance and delaying tactics, the judge believed his story about losing his job and having no money and let him off the hook. Not only that, but after all the aggravation the judge took less than ten minutes to decide on doing nothing.

Many such women will abandon their efforts to pursue child support when they realize how difficult and frustrating the process can be.

Finally, there are still other women who have never taken steps to get a child support order. Some are women whose children were born out of wedlock; because they never married they erroneously believe that their children are not entitled to child support. Others fail to secure an award because they feel disgraced, do not want to get involved with the legal system, or would rather rely on their family for support. In the latter group are those who choose not to have any relationship between father and child and decline support in order to prevent such a relationship. This includes women who never even tell the father that he has a child.

> Katherine came from a background of some means and education. When she became pregnant she felt that she had disgraced her family. She was deeply ashamed, but they were against abortion and encouraged her to have the baby. The last thing she wanted was to call attention to what she had done by trying to get the father to contribute financially. Her family agreed to help her out and she didn't need his money. What she did need, he was not going to give her anyway since he told her at the beginning of their brief relationship that he was not looking for anything serious. She decided that she would prevent any further disgrace by not even telling him about the child.

And there are single mothers who through their naiveté, passivity, inappropriate behavior, and feeling of lack of entitlement inadvertently contribute to their children's problems. Most single mothers, however, are deeply concerned about their children's welfare and would willingly, if not gladly, at least do what is needed in the best interest of the children.

WHAT A WOMAN CAN DO TO FACILITATE COMPLIANCE

In recent years state and federal governments have instituted significant new methods for locating delinquent fathers and making them meet their child support obligations (see chapter 5). It is clear, however, to anyone who has been involved in child support

collection that practical solutions are much more effective than
agency or judicial proceedings. Adversarial confrontations drain
everyone involved of precious and scarce time, energy, and money.
They may even have negative effects on the children by maintaining a high level of post divorce turmoil. Understanding the
delinquent father's motivation can sometimes be helpful in gain-
ing his compliance. The following are some ideas to keep in mind.

When there is a good relationship between ex-spouses, there
tends to be greater compliance with child support payments.
Assuming the custodial parent's goal is to ensure the best interests
of the children, and that compliance with child support obligations
promotes that goal, the first task is to establish and maintain as
good a relationship as possible. This may mean consciously
putting aside grudges and lingering feelings of anger toward an ex-
spouse. This is often not easy, since divorce is usually acrimonious
and leaves a legacy of bitterness and disappointment. Yet it is this
very lingering conflict during the post divorce stage that is often
used by the noncustodial father to rationalize his failure to make
payments. A woman seeking to ensure compliance with support
obligations should attempt to work through or set aside negative or
hostile feelings in order to minimize conflict with her ex-husband.
This is also likely to improve his relationship with the children,
which will also increase the likelihood of paying support.

It is important to reiterate here that an agreement reached
voluntarily by both parties is more likely to work than is one that
is ordered by the court without participation and agreement of the
parties. While it is important to formalize any private agreement
by presenting it in court, a mutually negotiated and voluntary
agreement is more likely to be honored by the parties. Once again,
this requires the parties to be able to set aside negative feelings,
focus the negotiation on the welfare of the children rather than
continuing pre-divorce conflicts, and to arrive at a child support
agreement that both parties feel has tried to accommodate their
needs.

While it may be important to settle such practical matters as how
and when child support payments will be made (e.g., by check

through the mail, by deposit made into a bank account, by electronic funds transfer, etc.), an important concern of fathers is that they be able to exercise a degree of control over their obligation. Sometimes those who feel little control will use this as a rationale for nonpayment. For example, if the children are older and it is important to the father to demonstrate to them that he contributes to their support in a significant way, he might make payments directly to their school, to extracurricular activities, or even purchase necessities himself.

Many noncustodial fathers also feel a loss of control over the decision-making process concerning both how their children will be raised and how the money that they pay will be used. Fathers frequently feel that their money goes into a "black hole" controlled by their ex-wife, who they often suspect uses it for herself and not the children. Whether these fears and suspicions are real or fabricated to avoid payment, often the result is that the children do not receive the support that is due. An instrument that has emerged to deal with this, as well as to negotiate a voluntary agreement, is mediation. Mediators are usually professionals trained in the art of negotiated settlements. A mediator can be hired by the parties or suggested by the court to devise a workable agreement. The mediator is not aligned with either party, but is engaged to facilitate accord. All parties have an opportunity to express themselves and to voice their needs and concerns. The process is intended to allay fears, deal with defensiveness and rationalization, create problem solving, and consider the needs of all the parties, particularly the best interests of the children. Child support agreements that are voluntarily established through mediation have higher rates of observance than those that are ordered by the court. Women who are concerned about compliance should make every effort to negotiate their own settlement and should be aware of the positive results obtained through mediation.

As emphasized throughout this book, another issue closely related to maintaining child support is the degree of emotional connection between a father and his children. If conditions become such that fathers lose their sense of closeness or connectedness with their children, the likelihood of their keeping up their support is diminished. This can occur as time goes by and the father sees less and less of his children because they get older and develop their own relationships. It can also occur if the father or children move far away from one another. It also happens to some men when they remarry and develop new allegiances and responsibilities. Regardless of the reason for the estrangement, the deterioration of the emotional connection between a father and his children significantly affects his commitment to their financial support. It is very important that the father be assisted in maintaining his relationship with his children. Regular visits are important. Having the father participate in decision making around important child issues is crucial. Both reinforce the bond between a father and his children.

Even if regular visitation or paternal participation is not feasible (or perhaps desirable), other steps can be taken to keep the father informed, and thus involved, with his children, albeit on a more superficial level. It is important to make every effort to keep him in touch with the children's development, their accomplishments, and their needs. Pictures can be sent regularly. The children themselves can send notes and memorabilia related to their interests and accomplishments. Every effort that keeps him in contact with his children will enhance the likelihood of their getting the child support to which they are entitled.

While a woman's first resort in collecting support is through the appropriate governmental agencies, keeping in mind the suggestions above, there is still an avenue of last resort. As a final attempt to secure payment, a woman can attempt the following suggestions and, in doing so, be more outrageous than the deadbeat dad. Such behavior is not recommended for the faint of heart or for those who are more concerned with not looking silly or being criticized. This approach requires that the woman be willing to be annoying, embarrassing, and persistent, for there are times when "the squeaky wheel" does not get the grease. For example, if the deadbeat's workplace is known, she might go there dressed in rags, perhaps with the children, making it known to all what the problem is and who is at fault. As long as no laws are broken, she can make her point in a powerful and effective manner. She might even picket the deadbeat's work place or home with signs letting people know that he has failed to live up to his legal and moral commitment to his children. This approach is clearly radical, and undoubtedly there will be those who will view these actions as validation for why the woman is alone and why her overtures are disregarded. Keeping in mind that one might be thought of as crazy, this approach should be considered when all other attempts have been unsuccessful.

There is no guarantee that such guerrilla tactics will work, but in the very least a struggling single parent whose children are being denied support can feel that she has done everything humanly and legally possible to take care of her children. In the final analysis, there may be some child support situations that cannot be resolved. After going through all the appropriate governmental channels, some deadbeat dads may have disappeared. Others, if discovered, may be unemployed or have another situation that makes it unlikely that child support will be forthcoming. And still others may be determined not to succumb to even the most creative and persistent efforts at provoking guilt, embarrassment, and humiliation. To persist in these situations may be futile; when it is clear that one is fighting a losing battle, then one should probably stop wasting resources and find more productive ways of using their energy to help the children.

8

Social Relationships, Economic Responsibility, and the Deadbeat Epidemic

INTRODUCTION

It seems clear that in today's world more and more individuals find that ethical obligation and legal responsibility lead to conflict about moral judgment and values. Marital obligations are readily accepted and easily dissolved; women are faced with ever more restrictions concerning their rights and access to reproductive choice. While sometimes men may have virtually no say at all in an abortion decision, men's casual and irresponsible sexual practices also produce large numbers of children without producing a parental sense of responsibility. The costs of childrearing have made even the traditional family upbringing a luxury, to say nothing of what is in store for those who attempt it under less-than-ideal circumstances.

Society is moving toward insisting upon greater parental obligation, and enforcing child support obligations has become a national priority. Having attempted to balance the rights of non-custodial parents and the children who must rely on them for basic support, the swing of the pendulum is now toward a system that looks to private support (from parents) as its first avenue of recourse and to public subsidy only as a means of last resort.

Does this society support this vision? Virtually no one disagrees that the upbringing and support of children is normally best left to the parents whose social bond and moral obligation goes a long way toward providing a healthy and productive upbringing. But the reality is that there are hundreds of thousands of unsupported or undersupported children in this, the wealthiest country in the world. Through no fault of their own, they bear the burden both of a failed marriage and failed social institutions. And if that isn't bad enough, they themselves eventually make the greatest contribution to perpetuating the failure: too large a portion of today's criminals, drug users, uneducated youth, and all-around societal dropouts are yesterday's neglected and abandoned children who, right from their beginning, never had much of a chance. So while society can refuse to assume public responsibility for a private obligation, it knows from experience that it eventually pays the price anyway. And this says nothing of the wasted human lives and the loss of human potential that occurs in the crossfire.

Does this mean that society should more willingly pick up the tab for the private folly of deadbeat parents? Here's something else to consider. The societal net cast by the various welfare programs attempts to help out anyone in genuine need, but its grasp is disproportionately on the youngest and oldest members of society. There has been great emphasis recently on the "graying" of America in recognition of the fact that people are living longer and that the elderly are comprising a larger proportion of the overall population. Who will be called upon to support tomorrow's increasingly elderly population? Today's children, of course. The same children about whom we debate whether society owes them a decent start in life. The stability and productivity of these children will be the insurance policy for our aging society that needs to be supported into perpetuity.

Stan and Marie are a professional couple who chose not to have children. Both were involved in busy careers and they had developed a comfortable lifestyle of travel, expensive taste, and too little time to attend to the chores of childrearing. Their income was modest but adequate to meet all of their needs. When Marie was sixty, she developed Alzheimer's disease and her condition deteriorated rapidly. Stan went through what little they had saved, and less than a year later Marie's care was paid through various social programs, primarily Social Security disability and Medicaid. Upon her death nearly eight years later, Marie had run up nursing home bills in excess of $700,000, funded by Medicaid and paid for by taxpayers. These people, of course, were the generation of other people's children.

The analogy of today's children to the elderly is appropriate for another reason as well. Today the primary means of support for the elderly is the social welfare system, including Medicare, Medicaid, Social Security, and other social programs. While at one time the elderly used to look first to their families, and particularly their children, for support in their declining years, today society has accepted that responsibility. And it has come to be an enormous responsibility—to the tune of hundreds of billions of dollars each year. While the answer is not to abandon the needy elderly, it becomes clear that the more politically vocal populations (able to advocate for themselves) are able to benefit greatly from generous social programs, while in many respects society has fallen short on behalf of its children.

For women, the instability of marriage (currently, about 50 percent of new marriages end in divorce) creates a substantial burden for many who would choose home over career in a different era. Even with the present social support system and its increasingly rigorous attempts at enforcement, having children is still a gamble. Doubtless the greater emphasis on pursuing biological fathers has led to many responsible men protecting themselves from unwanted pregnancies. Thus the trend is for many of the more responsible adults to decide not to bring children into the world if they are not prepared to care for them. Many more children are being born to those least equipped or prepared to care for them. A substantially increased number of married couples are choosing to remain childless or produce fewer children, largely because of the instability of relationships and the enormous cost of raising a family.

> Susan and Len married in their twenties. Both maintained blue-collar jobs and together their incomes were sufficient, but not excessive, to maintain a modest lifestyle. When they considered children, it became clear that even one child would be an economic burden, particularly if Susan were to stop working. But desiring a child and willing to make the sacrifice, Susan considered realistically the consequences of having a child, particularly if the marriage broke up at some point in the future. Ultimately she determined that it would be virtually impossible for Len to support her and a child and two households, as they were currently just making ends meet on two incomes and one household. Seeing no reasonable likelihood of greater income potential and understanding the reality of failed marriages, she ultimately decided to forego childbearing.

At some point the decline in reproduction, particularly by the more responsible members of society, will severely impact the economy and drive down its ability to maintain even the status quo. Today it is estimated that nearly 25 percent of all children live under the poverty line and that nearly 50 percent of black children fall into that category. These neglected and impoverished children are the products of failed private responsibility plus a society that is too overburdened to assume its share of the obligation. Failure to support today's children deprives the next generation of healthy, educated, productive people who will go on to maintain the social support system. Nearly everyone is somehow dissatisfied with public expenditures, but the time is ripe to reconsider whether it is prudent to skimp in an area where the welfare of needy children is at stake.

To suggest that society owes more of a debt to its underprivileged children does not in any way condone the actions of able parents who abdicate their responsibility. Certainly biological (or adoptive) parents should be required to assume as much of the financial responsibility for their children as they can. At present, however, social intervention has been inadequate to keep large numbers of children above the poverty line—a minimal standard that is well below what a child needs to be raised decently.

HELPING THE CUSTODIAL PARENT

The deadbeat epidemic occurs within a context that is usually either a divorce, an out-of-wedlock pregnancy, or a similar situation wherein one parent not only provides the major source of support of the children but is also a sole custodian. Single parenting is an enormous burden on a working parent, who often needs more than economic support to assist in raising the children. But the absent parent doubtless has his story as well. All too often he has weak social ties to his children and few rights with respect to the major decisions that affect their lives. Courts specifically refuse to tie together child support with visitation in any way that would suggest that a man somehow must "pay" for the right to a relationship with his child. But there is an undeniable correlation between the social ties that a parent maintains with his children and his willingness to pay support. The question of whether a "mere" biological link to a child is adequate to impose such a heavy burden on an absent father is a difficult one. The difficulty is compounded by the reasons for the absence: a man who voluntarily chooses to absent himself from his children's lives might be treated differently from the man who is left behind when his children are removed from his reach.

What, if anything, can society do to ease the burden on the custodial parent and to assist absent fathers in staying in meaningful relationships with their children? Some reform has occurred in the work arena where flexible hours, parental leave, and similar programs have been geared toward enabling working parents to accommodate both the requirements of their jobs and the needs of their families. Various tax reforms have attempted to shift some of the burden away from families that can barely make ends meet. But much more remains to be done.

What about absent fathers who want to establish or maintain significant social ties with their children? More and more courts are willing to order joint child custody in cases where it appears to be workable. Recognizing both the emotional need for a child to maintain a bond with two parents and the increased likelihood of an absent parent paying support, a "presumption" of joint child custody actually exists in some states. By the same token, courts are also more willing to recognize alternative life styles and to accommodate the needs of, for example, gay and lesbian parents who want to continue significant bonds with their children.

> Todd and Marianne divorced less than three years after they married. Todd revealed that he was a gay man and that it was difficult for him to be married to Marianne. At the time of the divorce, the couple had twin daughters. Both parents sought custody. Notwithstanding Todd's sexual orientation, the court ordered that the couple attempt joint custody, including shared physical custody. The children spent several days each week in the home of first one parent and then the other. Each parent contributed significantly to the support of the children, both while in their custody and for extraordinary expenses.

While at one time homosexuality was considered a bar to child custody, many courts today are willing to view the "best interests" of the children in totality. Sexual orientation may play a role in the court's decision, but even courts recognize that the welfare of children is too important to be based upon outdated stereotypes or political agenda. The court's decision about child placement and entitlement to support is so crucial that the court must carefully weigh the evidence about what will and will not impact on the welfare of the children. This means, for example, that a court cannot ignore the relationship between a divorced parent's continued social ties with the children and a parent's willingness to contribute to the children's economic needs. It also means that courts must acknowledge that a parent is no less a parent because of marital status or sexual orientation. A parent has a special and unique connection to the child that is unlikely to be duplicated in any subsequent relationship. A court decision that unnecessarily alienates a parent and child can do irreparable harm. Custody, visitation, and support are inextricably tied together. They cannot each be viewed in a vacuum.

DIRECTIONS FOR THE FUTURE

Much remains to be done on behalf of children who do not have the benefit of two-parent families and on behalf of the parents who struggle to give their children a decent start in life under less-than-ideal circumstances. With respect to single custodial parents, mothers and fathers alike, the greatest assistance they need is usually in the employment area. Since most must work to support themselves and their children, they need employment practices that assist them in reentering the work force after having parented. Some seek jobs years later in life, with outdated skills and, of course, fewer years of potential service than their youthful competitors. Many require flexible schedules in order to accommodate their parental obligations. Some have day care needs. Many require time off when their children are sick or have obligations of their own. Still others require special accommodations limiting out-of-town travel and evening obligations. Today the work force, in large measure, still frowns on workers who cannot be completely dedicated to the job because of conflicting obligations. Clearly one answer must lie in restructuring private enterprise (and public employers as well) such that parenting obligations are viewed as such worthy and honorable activities that employers are

willing to assist workers in meaningful ways. The seeds of greater
flexibility have been sown, but much remains to be done.

On behalf of noncustodial parents, often fathers, more needs to
be done to help them establish and maintain their ties with their
children, even if from a distance. Joint or shared custody is one
incentive, but clearly it needs to be tempered by what is best,
overall, for the children. A parent who will only pay support in
exchange for custody may be a less-than-ideal custodian. On the
other hand, the reality is that once families separate, some members move away, remarry, or become estranged by bitterness so
that meaningful relationships between parent and child are difficult. And once this emotional bond is severed, the probability of
reliable financial support diminishes sharply.

Arguably the most difficult task to accomplish is to enforce the
economic obligations of biological fathers who do not acknowledge their parental status and who are called upon to pay support
only after a paternity proceeding or similar confrontation requires
them to do so. Children who are the products of casual sexual
practices, teenage pregnancies, or other situations where paternity
is denied or where there is an unwillingness to accept parental
obligations, have the least chance of having their economic needs
fulfilled. Sometimes the circumstances that give rise to these
pregnancies are such that we are even left with sympathy for the
fathers.

Erin was born to an unmarried couple who were barely
more than children themselves. They had little intention of making a long-term commitment to each other
and less intention of having a child. In fact, most of the
time they were cautious and used birth control and
even discussed their willingness to have an abortion in
the event of an accident. When Jan found out she was
pregnant, Dick was willing to support her through the
abortion and use what little money he had to pay all of
the expenses. Arrangements were made, but when the
time actually came, Jan simply could not go through

with it. Erin was born seven months later. Dick, age twenty and trying to finish college, has never been able to find out why Jan wouldn't go through with the abortion or even whether the pregnancy was intentional.

Sarah had been having a sexual relationship with several men when she became pregnant. None knew of the others. During the pregnancy, she terminated her relationship with all of them without any meaningful explanations. Nearly two years later, she instituted a paternity proceeding and three men were identified as possible fathers. There were, in fact, two others, but she couldn't remember who they were and didn't know how to locate them. Of the three possible fathers, one was ruled out as not being a biological fit. The others, Glen and Chuck, were both found to be potential candidates, with Glen having a higher genetic probability. Glen had only had sex with Sarah once, and she considered him the least likely candidate for that reason. The court saw it differently and his paternity was established, almost as though by default.

Do passing acquaintances and casual sexual partners owe an obligation of support, which today is estimated in the range of $100,000 per child through the age of eighteen? Should a man have his whole life affected by a consensual act with an unintended consequence? Those who are inclined to answer in the negative are immediately posed with the dilemma of who should support these children. Are those who are sympathetic for the plight of the deadbeat dads willing to pay the bills for their unwanted offspring?

Finally, what about the women who choose not to disclose to a casual sex partner that a pregnancy was conceived? Some do not want to incur a lifelong obligation for an ongoing relationship with the child's father. They would rather raise the child alone than share the joys and burdens with a man who was merely a casual encounter. Others (perhaps those experienced with other deadbeat dads) prefer to pursue AFDC rather than take on the challenge of pursuing a deadbeat dad. At least to date, welfare payments are much more reliable and trouble free than the tribulations of chasing an unwilling father. These are some of the considerations that lead a single mother to choose AFDC over chasing a deadbeat dad. So far, the state and federal governments have allowed her to do so.

NEW DIRECTIONS

In a day and age where the federal budget is overburdened and compelling crises exist all over the world, it is difficult to convince lawmakers that yet even more money should be allocated to the needy children whose deadbeat dads are simply not providing them with adequate support. And yet the country (and, indeed, the world) has no greater resource than its children who, without question, comprise its future. Today the Republican majority in both houses of Congress has included within its Contract with America a reform of the welfare system, including AFDC. Among its mandates is the determination to pursue delinquent fathers, with an important first step and top priority being to identify them. Thus the Republican answer to casual relationships is clearly one of responsibility: Thou shalt support the child thou dost father. There is no room for error, and no accommodation for men who, through ignorance or deception, conceive unwanted children. Today the country just simply cannot afford otherwise.

Is there a better way of striking a balance between taxpayer burden, child poverty, and the other unmet needs of children that result from the deadbeat epidemic? Any solution that does not place the brunt of the economic burden on a child's parents is destined to fail. The children, inevitably caught in the crossfire, are the ones least able to advocate for themselves: they cannot vote; they cannot assemble or picket; many cannot attend to even their own most basic needs. Their despair, dependency, and antisocial behavior is their only manner of protest. Every new political administration promises to balance the needs of these children with those of a society overburdened with social programs. Welfare reforms in general, and deadbeat dads in particular, have been identified as among the greatest priorities today. Aggressive, tenacious, and consistent efforts to have full child support payments made must be accomplished through strong federal and state enforcement policies and procedures. Modern technology allows for the use of varieties of databases such as: income tax information, Social Security, drivers' licenses, and other forms of licensing and registrations, to be used to track deadbeats. Information can be shared between federal and state agencies so that crossing state lines can no longer be used to avoid responsibility. Even noncustodial parents who are unemployed can share their unemployment benefits or workers' compensation payments with their children through the automatic withholding of support payments. Those delinquent parents who continue to refuse to comply with their child support obligations should be swiftly punished by having their licenses revoked and their wages and tax refunds garnished. Ultimately they should face a jail sentence. We must send the message that a parent's non-support of children will no longer be tolerated. With changes in social policy we hope that these parents can be persuaded, one way or another, to assume greater responsibility for their children.

Bibliography

American Bar Association. *America's Children at Risk: A National Agenda for Legal Action.* Chicago: American Bar Association Journal, 1993.

Anand, G. "3 Charged with Evasion of Child Support Bills; Fathers Allegedly Owe $200,000 Total." *Boston Globe,* June 2, 1994, 34.

Arditti, J.A., and K.R. Allen. "Understanding Distressed Fathers' Perceptions of Legal and Relational Inequities." *Post-Divorce Family and Conciliation Courts Review* 31(4):461-76, 1993.

Bautz, B.J., and R.M. Hill. "Mediating the Breakup: Do Children Win?" *Mediation Quarterly* 8(3):199-210, 1991.

Bossin, P. "How to Handle Custody Cases." *Trial* 28(6):24-28, 1992.

Boston Globe. "Child Support Collections Higher." January 7, 1994, 12.

———. "Law Said to Help Dads Shirk Debt." February 9, 1994, 72.

———. " 'Deadbeat' RI Dad Free After Court Settlement." May 4, 1994, 91.

———. "Welfare Fathers." August 8, 1994, 2.

———. "Lottery Winner, Ex-Wife Reach Settlement." August 24, 1994, 80.

———. "Deadbeat Parents Owe $34b, Study Says." October 31, 1994, 1.

———. "Clinton Urges License Revocation in Child-Support Cases." March 19, 1995, 3.

———. "Agencies Toughen Efforts to Collect Child Support." April 11,

1995, 4.

The Boston Globe Sunday Magazine. "A Dead-Beat Dad's Story."
March 26, 1995, 22.

Braver, S.L., S.A. Wolchik, I.N. Sandler, V.L. Sheets, et al. "A
Longitudinal Study of Non-Custodial Parents: Parents Without
Children." *Journal of Family Psychology Special Section: Fami-
lies in Transition* 7(1):9-23, 1993.

Brenner, L., and R. Stern. *Getting Your Share.* New York: Signet, 1989.

Bulcroft, K., and R. Bulcroft. "The Timing of Divorce: Effects on Parent-
Child Relationships in Later Life." *Research on Aging* 13(2):226-
43, 1991.

Burchinal, L. "Characteristics of Adolescents from Unbroken and Re-
constituted Family." *Journal of Marriage and the Family* 26:44-
51, 1964.

Coleman, M. , and L.H. Ganong. "Financial Responsibility for Children
Following Divorce and Remarriage." *Journal of Family and
Economic Issues Special Issue: Toward the Turn of the Century:
Families and Economic Realities* 13(4):445-55, 1992.

Dedent, P. "Establishing and Enforcing the Child Support Obligation: An
Evaluation of Practical Impediments to an Effective System."
Capital University Law Review 19:1169, 1990.

Duncan, S.W. "Economic Impact of Divorce on Children's Development: Current Findings and Policy Implications." *Journal of
Clinical Child Psychology* 23:444-57, 1994.

English, B. "This Charles Is No Prince." *Boston Globe,* February 9,
1994, 17.

Fassel, D. *Growing Up Divorced: A Road to Healing for Adult Children
of Divorce.* New York: Pocket, 1991.

Furstenberg, F.F.; S.P. Morgan; and P.D. Allison. "Paternal Participation
and Children's Well-Being After Marital Dissolutions." *American Sociological Review* 52(5):695-701, 1987.

Goode, W. *After Divorce.* New York: Free Press, 1956.

Goodman, E. "No Deadbeats at the Wheel." *Boston Globe,* July 28, 1994,
11.

Grant, T. "Deadbeat Dad's Payment from Lottery is Frozen." *Boston
Globe,* April 20, 1994, 26.

Grunwald, M. "Jackpot Winner Sued by Ex-Wife; Alimony Demanded
After 48-Year Rift." *Boston Globe,* July 19, 1994, 20.

Guidubaldi, J.; H.K. Cleminshaw; J.D. Perry; and C.S. McLoughlin.

"The Impact of Parental Divorce on Children: Report of the Nationwide NASP Study." Presented at the annual convention of the National Association for School Psychologists, March 1983.

Haynes, M.C. "Child Support and the Courts in the Year 2000." *American Journal of Trial Advocacy* 17:693, 1994.

Haynes, M.C., and G.D. Dodson. *Interstate Child Support Remedies.* Washington, DC: U.S. Department of Health and Human Services, 1990.

Hetherington, E.M.; M. Cox; and R. Cox. "Divorced Fathers." *Family Coordinator* 25:417-28, 1976.

———. "Effects of Divorce on Parents and Children." In *Non-Traditional Families: Parenting and Child Development,* edited by M.E. Lamb, 233-88, Hillsdale, NJ: Lawrence Erlbaum, 1982.

———. "Long-Term Effects of Divorce and Remarriage on the Adjustment of Children." *Journal of the American Academy of Child Psychiatry* 24:518-30, 1985.

Hetherington, E.M.; M. Stanley-Hagen; and E.R. Anderson. "Marital Transitions: A Child's Perspective." *American Psychologist* 44(2):303-12, 1989.

Howe, P. "New 'Deadbeat Dad' Law Massachusetts Child Support Statistics." *Boston Globe,* January 21, 1994, 18.

———. "15-Year Old Son of No. 1 'Deadbeat Dad' Pleads for Support; 10 Most Wanted 'Deadbeat Dads.' " *Boston Globe,* April 28, 1994, 32.

Jackson, P., and N. Runyon. "Caring for Children from Divorced Families." *American Journal of Maternal and Child Nursing* 2:126, 1983.

Kaye, D.H., and R. Kanwischer. "Admissibility of Genetic Testing in Paternity Litigation: A Survey of State Statutes." *Family Law Quarterly* 22:109, 1988.

Keith, R. "Interception of Federal Tax Refunds: An Update on Litigation and Program Development." *Improving Child Support Practice* 2, 1986.

Kelly, R., and B. Berg. "Measuring Children's Reactions to Divorce." *Journal of Clinical Psychology* 34:215-24, 1978.

Kahn, A.J., and S.B. Kamerman. *Child Support: From Debt Collection to Social Policy.* Newbury Park, CA: Sage, 1988.

King, V. "Nonresident Father Involvement and Child Well-Being: Can Dads Make a Difference?" *Journal of Family Issues* 15(1):78-96,

1994.

Krantzler, M., and M. Belli. *Divorcing.* New York: St. Martin's, 1988.

Kurdek, L.A. "Custodial Mothers' Perceptions of Visitation and Payment of Child Support by Noncustodial Fathers in Families with Low and High Levels of Preseparation Interparental Conflict." *Journal of Applied Developmental Psychology* 7(4):307-23, 1986.

Levin, M.L. "Sequelae to Marital Disruption in Children." *Journal of Divorce and Remarriage* 12(2-3):25-80, 1989.

Long, N., and R. Foreland. "The Effects of Parental Divorce and Parental Conflict on Children: An Overview." *Developmental and Behavioral Pediatrics* 8(5):292, 1987.

Mandell, R. "Use of Mediation in Child Support Disputes." *Mediation Quarterly* 17:33-37, 1987.

New York Times. "Divorced Fathers Make Gains in Battles to Increase Rights." April 26, 1995, A1.

Nichols-Casebolt, A., and S.K. Danziger. "The Effect of Childbearing Age on Child Support Awards and Economic Well-Being Among Divorcing Mothers." *Journal of Divorce* 12(4):35-48, 1989.

Nuta, V.R. "Emotional Aspects of Child Support Enforcement." *Family Relations Journal of Applied Family and Child Studies* 35(1):177-81, 1986.

Nye, F. "Child Adjustment in Broken and in Unhappy Unbroken Homes." *Marriage and Family Living* 19:356-61, 1957.

Oppawsky, J. "Family Dysfunctional Patterns During Divorce—From the View of the Children." *Journal of Divorce and Remarriage* 12(2-3):139-52, 1989.

Pearson, J., and J. Anhalt. "Examining the Connection Between Child Access and Child Support." *Family and Conciliation Courts Review* 32(1):93-109, 1994.

Peters, D., and R.L. Strom. *Divorce and Child Custody.* Scottsdale, AZ: Makai, 1992.

Peterson, J.L., and N. Zill. "Marital Disruption, Parent/Child Relationships and Behavioral Problems in Children." Presented at the annual meeting of the Society for Research in Child Development, April 1983.

Rakowsky, J. "U.S. Chases Doctor for Nonsupport of Mass. Girl, 10." *Boston Globe,* July 15, 1994, 19.

Roberts, P. *Childhood's End.* Uniondale, NY: Child Support Assurance

Consortium, 1993.

Runyon, N., and P.L. Jackson. "Divorce: Its Impact on Children." *Perspectives in Psychiatric Care* 23(3-4):101-5, 1987/88.

Sales, B.; R. Mamber; and L. Rothman. "Social Science Research and Child Custody Decision Making." *Applied and Preventive Psychology* 1(1):23-40, 1992.

Secor, G. "Michael H. vs Gerald D.: Due Process and Equal Protection Rights of Unwed Fathers." *Hastings Constitutinal Law Quarterly* 17:759, 1990.

Seltzer, J.A., and Y. Brandreth. "What Fathers Say About Involvement with Children After Separation." *Journal of Family Issues* 15(1):49-77, 1994.

Stephen, E.H.; V.A. Freedman; and J. Hers. "Near and Far: Contact of Children with Their Nonresidential Fathers." *Journal of Divorce and Remarriage* 20(3-4):171-91, 1993.

Teachman, J.D. "Contributions to Children by Divorced Fathers." *Social Problems* 38(3):358-71, 1991.

Umberson, D., and C.L. Williams. "Divorced Fathers: Parental Role Strain and Psychological Distress." *Journal of Family Issues* 14(3):378-400, 1993.

U.S. Commission on Interstate Child Support. *Supporting Our Children: A Blueprint for Reform.* Washington, DC: U.S. Government Printing Office, 1992.

U.S. Department of Commerce. *Statistical Abstract of the United States.* Washington, DC: U.S.Government Printing Office, 1994.

Veum, J.R. "The Relationship Between Child Support and Visitation: Evidence from Longitudinal Data." *Social Science Research* 22(3):229-44, 1993.

Wall, J.C. "Maintaining the Connection: Parenting as a Noncustodial Father." *Child and Adolescent Social Work Journal* 9(5):441-56, 1992.

Wallerstein, J. *Surviving the Break-Up: How Children and Parents Cope with Divorce.* New York: Basic Books, 1980.

———. "Children of Divorce: Preliminary Report of a Ten-Year Follow-Up of Older Children and Adolescents." *Journal of the American Academy of Child Psychiatry* 24:545-53, 1985.

Whitehead, B.D. "Dan Quayle Was Right." *Atlantic Monthly* 271(4):47-84, 1993.

Wright, D.W., and S.J. Price. "Court-Ordered Child Support Payment:

The Effect of the Former-Spouse Relationship on Compliance."
Journal of Marriage and the Family 48(4):869-74, 1986.
Zeanah, P.D. "Children of Divorce." *Issues in Comprehensive Pediatric
Nursing* 6:91-106, 1983.

Index

About the Authors

MARCIA MOBILIA BOUMIL is a faculty member of the School of Medicine, Tufts University. Boumil is the author of numerous articles and books including *Law, Ethics and Reproductive Choice* (1994) and, with Joel Friedman, *Betrayal of Trust* (Praeger, 1995).

JOEL FRIEDMAN is a licensed psychologist who has served for the past 20 years on the faculty of the Harvard Medical School. He is author and coauthor of several books including *Betrayal of Trust*, with Boumil (Praeger, 1995).

DATE DUE

~~MAR 3 0 1997~~	~~MAR 0 3 1998~~
~~MAR 1 8 1998~~	~~APR 1 5 1998~~
~~MAR 2 1998~~	MAY 1 2 2005

GAYLORD

PRINTED IN U.S.A.